Marxist Film Theory and *Fight Club*

Marxist Film Theory and *Fight Club*

ANNA KORNBLUH

BLOOMSBURY ACADEMIC
NEW YORK • LONDON • OXFORD • NEW DELHI • SYDNEY

BLOOMSBURY ACADEMIC
Bloomsbury Publishing Inc
1385 Broadway, New York, NY 10018, USA
50 Bedford Square, London, WC1B 3DP, UK

BLOOMSBURY, BLOOMSBURY ACADEMIC and the Diana logo are
trademarks of Bloomsbury Publishing Plc

First published in the United States of America 2019
Reprinted 2020

For legal purposes the Acknowledgments on p. vi constitute an
extension of this copyright page.

Cover design by Alice Marwick
Cover images: Karl Marx portrait © johan10 / iStock. Fight Club, 1999,
Brad Pitt and Edward Norton © Everett Collection / Mary Evans.

Bloomsbury Publishing Inc does not have any control over, or
responsibility for, any third-party websites referred to or in this book.
All internet addresses given in this book were correct at the time of
going to press. The author and publisher regret any inconvenience
caused if addresses have changed or sites have ceased to exist,
but can accept no responsibility for any such changes.

Library of Congress Cataloging-in-Publication Data:
Names: Kornbluh, Anna.
Title: Marxist film theory and Fight club / Anna Kornbluh.
Description: New York, NY: Bloomsbury Academic, 2019. | Series: Film theory
in practice | Includes bibliographical references and index.
Identifiers: LCCN 2019007181 (print) | LCCN 2019012014 (ebook) | ISBN
9781501347313 (ePub) | ISBN 9781501347320 (ePDF) | ISBN 9781501347306
(pbk. : alk. paper) | ISBN 9781501347290 (hardback : alk. paper)
Subjects: LCSH: Film criticism. | Marxist criticism. | Motion
pictures–Philosophy. | Fight club (Motion picture)
Classification: LCC PN1995 (ebook) | LCC PN1995 .K67 2019 (print) |
DDC 791.4301–dc23
LC record available at https://lccn.loc.gov/2019007181

ISBN: HB: 978-1-5013-4729-0
PB: 978-1-5013-4730-6
ePDF: 978-1-5013-4732-0
eBook: 978-1-5013-4731-3

Series: Film Theory in Practice

Typeset by Deanta Global Publishing Services, Chennai, India
Printed and bound in the U.S.A. by Sheridan, Chelsea, Michigan

To find out more about our authors and books visit www.bloomsbury.com
and sign up for our newsletters.

CONTENTS

ACKNOWLEDGMENTS

I am grateful to the Bloomsbury Film Theory in Practice series editors Katie Gallof and Todd McGowan for the chance to write this book, which was more than usually fun. Teaching is the critic's everyday exercise of engaging publics, so I thank my hard-working, high-achieving undergraduate and graduate students at the University of Illinois at Chicago for their commitment. Special thanks are due to Justin Raden for inspiration and manuscript assistance. Writing, like film, is a social practice; I deeply appreciate the conversations with and feedback from many treasured interlocutors in Marxism and aesthetic theory, including Sianne Ngai, Jodi Dean, Leigh Claire La Berge, Julie Wilson, Hilary Neroni, Russell Sbriglia, Clint Burnham, and Matthew Flisfeder. Some of my earliest teachers—Doug Kellner, Kiarina Kordela, Ken Reinhard, Julia Reinhard Lupton, Etienne Balibar, and Slavoj Žižek—inspired my first thoughts about *Fight Club* in 1999, and these pages bear their imprint. I thank David Fincher and his cast and crew for creating a dynamic artwork to think with. And again, there is Todd McGowan, who took a chance eighteen years ago on an MA student with unruly ideas about film. In his brilliance and generosity, I have found a constant support and a perpetual muse.

Introduction

Marxism is . . . fill in the blank from where you sit. Because a sentence like that can only be finished from a particular point of view. College students in the United States in 2018 would have one answer, Labour Party officials in Britain another, unemployed youth in Spain another, Fox News commentators yet another. And that is one of the very first lessons that Karl Marx himself sought to impart: definitions, descriptions, analyses, representations cannot be impartial. Words, interpretations, ideas, and art issue from specific contexts, and often reflect the interests of specific subject positions. Moreover, this reflection does not result in a plurality of equal, competing ideas, but rather, some ideas emerge as dominant, and those will generally be the ideas that correspond to prevailing relations of power and wealth. As Marx put it in one of his very first programmatic essays laying out his break with conventional philosophy, "The ruling ideas in every epoch are the ideas of the ruling class." What made his philosophy novel was this commitment to tracking the relations of power and wealth that constitute the backdrop against which ideas are produced and disseminated. Philosophy before Marx might have thought of itself as a neutral birds-eye-view project, but Marx's intervention started from an insistence that philosophy is always invested in its own social situation, and that a philosophy which does not query its own investments is a philosophy that tacitly if not overtly endorses the social status quo.

Marxism starts with scrutinizing the social context of ideas, including whether philosophies pay attention to their own social context. But beyond this work of contextualizing, Marxism is also a project of intervening, of *transforming* the social context. Marx's context, mid-nineteenth-century Europe, was rapidly transforming due to industrial technology (machines, steam, factories), urbanization (the mass migration of people to urban centers to work in factories), and democratization (the legal restructuring of political rights to incorporate non-property-owners, women, and immigrants). Marx saw the potential of these transformations—a trajectory toward freedom from necessity—and he saw their actuality: immiseration of masses of people, overworked, overcrowded, under-actualized. Contradictions like that, between promise and reality, between future and present, between social facts looked at one way and social facts looked at another way— were the main object of his philosophic analysis. He wanted to make contradictions perceptible, thinkable, historicizable; and he thought it would be impossible for any philosopher or author or artist to take up a position without contradiction. Either they could deny contradictions, in which case they were likely trying to promote the smooth functioning of the status quo, or they could avow contradictions, in which case they would include the contradictory status of their own position.

For his part, Marx avowed the contradictions in the social relations of capitalism, and he took a side. The primary contradiction, what he also called the "simplest," is the antagonism between the capitalists and the workers. Capitalists control the means of production, and workers are the means of production. "Production" to Marx meant not just making goods in a factory, but also making the very conditions of human existence. Humans are animals who confront nature and are driven to produce transformations in it; who need one another to survive but don't fall into any natural framework for that interdependence. We need to make things, and we need to make our relations to one another. Production is a universal activity at this most general level: the activities that sustain our existence. Yet all human societies and all points in history configure production in very particular ways. Marx's primary insight is that these particular configurations of the universal are contingent, the outcome of choice and chance rather than the expression of nature. Contingent configurations can therefore be named and relativized, and human freedom may ultimately hinge upon deliberately directing contingency. Marx wants to name "the capitalist mode of production" (a phrase he used far more often than the plain word "capitalism") so that its contingency can come into the light, and so that other modes of production can become thinkable. The capitalist mode of production is distinguished—from the feudal mode, the socialist mode, the communist mode, and what he problematically calls "the Asiatic mode"—by its principle of wealth accumulation and surplus extraction, and by the theoretical freedom of labor it enables. The capitalist mode of production is organized to amass wealth through the activity of the many and to concentrate that mass in the hands of the few. The essential contradiction in capitalism is between these many and these few, the workers whose labor creates value and the owners whose social power enables them to capture that value. Wealth is the concrete form of the abstraction "value," an idea that humans invented to regulate their activities. The distribution of wealth in capitalism works unevenly: most people get income (with the chance to accumulate wealth) from working, but the rich minority get income from owning (employing workers, owning land, owning technology, owning stocks). The workers are a class of people, the owners are an opposing class of people, and struggle between the classes is paramount. To see this opposition in our own context is particularly clarifying: in the drastically polarized distribution of the early twenty-first century, 1 percent of the global population owns more than the bottom 90 percent put together.

Theorizing fundamental social contradictions like that between the ruling class and the working class involves tracing how contradictions manifest in most aspects of social life, from economic production to philosophical notions, from political institutions to cultural arts. This attention to the ubiquitous manifestation of contradiction accounts for the ongoing salience of Marxism and its extrapolation to new topics. Marx theorized contradictions in the nineteenth century, but his analytic tools remain powerful in the twenty-first century. Even though he lived before the development of economic ideologies like neoliberalism or cultural technologies like cinema, his framework of contradiction proves applicable and revealing.

Philosophers call this framework "dialectics." G. W. F. Hegel, a key influence for Marx, defined dialectics as a method of "the grasping of opposites in their unity or of the positive in the negative."[1] Dialectics is a method of avowing and theorizing contradiction. This means acknowledging opposing tendencies in a concrete situation, allowing contrasting possibilities in hypotheses, and proceeding from one observation or notion toward others by means of apprehending the tensions within the starting points. Rather than examine something in its decisive difference from everything else, dialectics puts an emphasis on relations and connections that provide context for the identity of the thing, on what something is in the process of becoming, and on how something is never fully identical to itself. Other philosophers, from Heraclitus and Socrates to Hegel and Schiller, and even to Marx's frequent coauthor Engels, have emphasized the universality of dialectics—its applicability to all phenomena in a world in which even nature effectuates an interpenetration of opposites. For Marx, however, who always insists on the context for ideas, dialectics is the method of inquiry that corresponds to capitalism, a social system of contradictions. This correspondence is itself—surprise!—dialectical: the contradictions of capitalism determine that philosophy in capitalism will be symptomatically contradictory, and at the same time, the ability to grasp contradictions is indispensable to taking critical distance from capitalism's contradictions.

The dialectical approach maintains that the critic is situated in a context, that the object of their critique is also situated, and that at the same time both the subject and object can transcend their context. Marx was a perpetual outsider (born Jewish in a Catholic town in a majority Protestant country, a native German who suffered Prussian oppression and lived in political exile in Belgium, France, and England, a member of a professionally aspirant class by birth but a member of an indebted precarious class by choice) who trained his sights on the constitutive *inside* of modern society, its fundamental structures and tendencies. His ideas extend beyond his context because they focus not just on context but on human universals like the creative production of existence and the necessity to create new contexts. This very energy of reflecting on human creativity endows art and artistic expression with a special significance within Marxism. For this reason—though also for others—Marxist philosophy may be more commonly embraced today in the study of cultural arts than in the study of economics or politics. This book takes up one such arena of cultural study—film and film theory—with the goal of invigorating both film studies and Marxist theory. We will introduce some key concepts in Marxist theory that are useful for understanding film, review some of the major film theories influenced by Marx, and practice Marxist film theory through interpreting the contemporary classic film *Fight Club* (David Fincher, 1999). After reading the book, you should be able to conduct your own Marxist theoretical analysis of other movies and even of related cultural products like television, music videos, photography, and novels. The tools of Marxist theory are helpful for understanding the arts we consume and enjoy every day, and the ways that consumption adds up to a culture. They are also helpful for mapping out the power interests of dominant culture and for thinking about strategies for transforming society. *Fight Club* explores the experience of dominant culture and possibilities for social transformation, so it serves this book not only as an example for Marxist theoretical exercises but also as a contribution to that theory.

This reciprocal dynamic whereby Marxist theory can enhance our understanding of cinema and cinema can enhance our understanding of Marxist theory is an example of dialectics. Throughout this book, we will pursue contradictions and their dialectical interpretation. Marxism is not just the contextualizing of film with respect to the class struggle; it is also the affirmation of the elementary human activities of creative production. Marxist film theory must therefore attend to contradictions such as the capacity of mass culture to both pacify the masses and express the necessity for their liberation, or the capacity of film production to both extend and challenge the capitalist mode of production. It must ask questions like how does the medium of cinema handle or even exploit the contradictory role of dominant cultural production? Do Hollywood films, produced by the ruling class, for the profit of the ruling class, ever betray their class interests? Can film be an art of contradiction?

To open this last question in particular, let us introduce some affinities between Marxism and film theory. The Marxist project of knowing the position from which one knows is interestingly intertwined with the medium of cinema since both are experiences of spectatorship. Theory, from the Greek *theorein*, meaning to look at or behold, is the movement from seeing an object to speculating about an object, endeavoring to understand its essence. All theory is thus, at some level, a practice of spectating. Marx's theory looks at how philosophy works in the world. Film theory looks at film, including the medium itself, its production, and the experience of spectatorship. It tries to fundamentally define the medium of film. What is film? How does a spectator encounter film differently from other arts? How does a film work differently than other modes of art? What does film do in the world? As theories of art since Plato have reckoned with the relationship between art and reality, film theory asks whether film has a special connection to, and special disconnection from, the "reality" we generally think of as distinct from art.

Film theory is wide-reaching and has many incarnations, perhaps because it curiously intensifies the very project of theory: theory is looking; film theory is looking at looking. Prominent schools of film theory include feminism, psychoanalysis, auteurism, phenomenology, queer studies, narratology, and Marxism. While Marxism is just one kind of film theory, one thesis of this book is that the basic tenets of Marxism should be foundational for all kinds of film theory. The theory of cinema, since its earliest incarnations, has been concerned with questions at the center of Marxist theory: What do human beings create when they work? Why do human beings create art in addition to working? What is the form of a work of art? How is a work of art produced? How is it consumed? In what ways is it ideological? In what ways is it autonomous? What are the industrial, technological, political, and economic conditions from which the work emerges? We understand cinema richly when we consider its form, its conditions of production, and its role in social relations, including the essential relationships of freedom and domination.

Both the theory of film and the analysis of film can be conducted from a Marxist perspective. Film *Theory* explores the medium of cinema in its specific difference from other media, and in its relationship to society. Film *Analysis* deploys the concepts developed in film theory to study the composition of particular films, using formal terms proper to the medium, like "cinematography," "editing," "mise-en-scène." Film Theory can help us understand an incredibly popular, incredibly rich medium, including the pleasures and power relations wrapped up with it. It can also help filmmakers understand their own labor, from the effects of their camera angles to the ramifications of their representations. In this way the theory itself can become part of the practice. Analysis of any given film might not explicitly address the questions of film theory, but versions of those questions (and versions of answers to them) are implicit in film analysis. When we analyze film, we consider cinematography, sound, lighting, setting, editing, and montage. We also consider acting and directing, the studio system, production expenses, sales statistics, and popularity. And of course we discuss story and plot. Emphasizing any of these considerations above others entails tacit decisions about the essence of cinema. Through dialectics, Marxism underscores the importance of making these decisions explicit, of interweaving analysis with theory, of yoking particular analysis of particular films to general theory of the cinematic medium and of social contradictions.

The universal language

The stress upon dialectics in the Marxist approach to film reflects the general character of the film medium itself, what has been celebrated as its "universal language." Because it began silently, but also because of the specific way in which film's immersive sensoria and diverse cultures can easily circulate with only a projector, film is thought to offer spectators the ability to participate in vastly differently worlds. Moreover, the cinema seems to intrinsically work toward a universal art, formally integrating prior media and types. According to one of its earliest theorists, Riccioto Canudo, cinema merges the types of media we usually think of as temporal (poetry, music, dance) with the spatial types (architecture, sculpture, and painting) and the result is a new heterogeneous and even paradoxical medium, a "plastic art in motion."[2] The nonverbal, integrative language of the cinema also strives toward universality in its blending of art and the world, and in its emanation from a collective, rather than an individual. Cinema combines the materials of film exposure with the material reality of the actors and setting in front of the camera, what is often called the "pro-filmic" event or referent. That is, while the events in a work of fiction can be understood as untethered from what actually exists in the world in which the author writes (no mother needs to die for Albert Camus to write "Mother died today" as the opening line of his novel *The Stranger*), cinema has generally, before the age of computer-generated imagery, necessitated that real actors or objects be arranged in particular ways in order to convey that an event is happening within a film. One very special aspect of the pro-filmic register of cinema is how necessarily collective it is, how many people are involved and how many different types of work they are carrying out. Camus may write his novel at his desk, but the director of a film must work in concert with actors, cinematographers, set designers, makeup artists, technicians, caterers, janitors, etc. Cinema is a medium, in other words, that is not just theoretically international and integrative, but also functionally communal and collaborative.

Along with these immersive, integrative, and collective features, film also convokes an international context. As Robert Stam notes, since its origins, film has been a medium practiced, produced, and consumed internationally: what began in the United States, Britain, and France (which were also the countries that invented photography) spread rapidly internationally, even to the developing world.[3] At the same time, the very sense of the world as an integrated system of nations is itself the product of particular developments in world politico-economic history, chiefly the ones for which Marxism endeavors to account: the advent of general standards for mercantile trade and contract law in the Treaty of Westphalia; the transatlantic slave trade; enclosure, defeudalization, and the emergence of wage labor; the development of the British Empire; massive population migrations to cities in the nineteenth century and across national boundaries in the twentieth century; the founding of the United Nations; and the ascension of multinational corporate conglomerates as the preeminent avenue of federation under globalization. These dynamics in the everyday practices and macro-history of the twentieth century, and their tendency toward integration of the world market, provide an important backdrop for the art of the cinema's claims to universality.

In its fundamentally social, fundamentally heterogeneous, and fundamentally integrated character, cinema arguably achieves at the dawn of the twentieth century the "total work of art" longed for by eighteenth- and nineteenth-century thinkers: a synthesis of art forms that actualizes human freedom. Marxist insights prompt us to understand that film's ability to do so is closely connected to its conditions of historical emergence: the rise of the cinema parallels the acme of the British Empire, that coordinated, violent, exploitative integration of much of three quarters of the world into a unified politico-economic system. The cinema first flourished in France, Britain, and the United States, the seats of imperial power. But this does not mean cinema is firstly or ultimately imperial. If art forms can not only symptomatize or diagnose their own conditions of production but also, in their energy as counter-factual and in their essence as creativity, gesture toward utopian horizons beyond those merely existing conditions, then the dialectical conclusion is that cinema is the paradigmatic artform of global capitalism *and* that it simultaneously points toward capitalism's unfulfilled promises of freedom and elective collectivity. *Fight Club*, we will come to see, can be analyzed as a symptomatic reproduction of its stage of global capitalism, as a diagnosis of that stage, and as a critical imaginative projection of stages to come. It is a testament to its complexity as a work of art that it occupies such contradictory ground.

The Marxist commitment to contextualizing cultural production enables thinking of art as something more situated and contingent than conventional paradigms hold. If in the history of philosophy prior to Marxian materialism art appears as creative expression and as the province of genius, the Marxist intervention dispels this appearance, centering the conditions of production as key for understanding art. The history of art therefore comes into view not as the advancement of genius in its quest for timeless expression, but as mutations in form and practice that track with transformations in the mode of production, and with techniques of the class struggle. Rather than tell the history of film, for instance, as the procession of brilliant directors, Marxists can tell the history of film with reference to macroeconomic factors like globalization, recessions, booms, and wage stagnation; to ideological formations like Fordism or neoliberalism; to industrial developments like the invention of sound technology, the advent of computer-generated animation, or the corporate consolidation of film studios with broader media companies and defense contractors. Most importantly, it can tell the history of film as the history of negotiating and aestheticizing contradictions.

This book is organized around two chapters, one which introduces Marxist theory and Marxist film theory, and the other which continues that theoretical exploration and the interpretative problems it poses by engaging with *Fight Club*. Due to the parameters of this Bloomsbury series, the focus on one film has skewed the theory toward Hollywood film, which occupies a hegemonic place in the universal language of film but is not representative of the global diversity of film practices. Similarly the theory chapter is in no way a comprehensive narrative of Marxism, but rather a schematization of some of the major concepts, motifs, and methods in both Marx's work and Marxist theorizing that connect to film theory. In some cases, these concepts have become central to film theory, but in other cases they have remained strangely peripheral. I have selected topics both because they are used in film theory and because I think they should be used more often—the core Marxist concepts continue to offer commanding avenues of exploration for the film classroom and the film student. Thus my overarching argument in Chapter 1 is that there can be more robust Marxist film theory. In Chapter 2, I position *Fight Club* as a contributor to that theory, arguing that the film itself makes thinkable many important Marxist topics, especially regarding the function of representation in the field of political-economic relations. This is not to say that the film itself is Marxist, but rather that the film itself is engaging in theorizing. Such esteem for the power of art is one of the many dialectical points I hope the book exemplifies.

CHAPTER ONE

Marxist Film Theory

In this chapter, I offer an overview of a few key concepts in Marxist theory that prove particularly foundational for the project of film theory, along with a summary of some of the ways those foundations have been built upon. The key concepts discussed are "mode of production," "ideology," and "mediation." Before turning to the outline of those key concepts, this chapter asserts in some broad strokes why Marxism in general is useful as a theoretical paradigm, since this cannot be taken for granted in academic inquiry at large nor in film studies at all. Resurgent interest in Marx after the global financial crisis of 2008 and the revaluing of socialist (albeit not communist) alternatives in 2016 and beyond suggest that the time is ripe for a renewed centrality of Marxism in film studies. Marxism is a project of composing new ideas in the service of composing a new social order, and that project remains compelling almost two hundred years after its emergence.

Formalism in Marxism

In the introduction, I indicated that through its emphasis on human creativity and the contingency of social history, Marxism can accord a special significance to art. I want to give that significance some more heft in pointing out how much Marxism defined itself as a philosophy of contradiction by analyzing the concrete forms in which contradiction takes shape. Indeed, "form" is a crucial category of analysis for Marx, and one which opens connections to aesthetics and to art interpretation. Marx presented his revolutions in thought as rooted in his focus on the *forms* of existing relations. He called this revolutionary approach "materialism." As he defines it, materialism addresses itself "first . . . to the existence of living human individuals . . . the organization of these individuals and their consequent relation to the rest of nature." Note the *plural* existence, and the organization of this plurality. Where Kant, Hegel, and other idealists philosophized in the singular, about being and consciousness and the idea, Marx pointed thought toward the ways that material context complicates, diversifies, and multiplies the singular subjects of philosophy. He contextualized philosophy's spiritual realm, placing ideas in their material context of power, relations, organizations, and the outcome of this process of contextualization was concern for the "definite forms" of philosophical abstractions. He differentiated between his philosophy and the prevailing idealist philosophy, and between his critique of economic relations and the prevailing discipline of bourgeois political economy, by training his gaze on the way phenomena are composed, arranged, designed, put together. Where bourgeois political economists before him had identified numerous aspects of capitalism and even promoted a labor theory of value, Marx distinguished his contribution to the critique of political economy with his own emphasis on what he called "forms" of value. *Capital*, Marx's culminating work, of course famously begins with the commodity form—"The wealth of those societies in which the capitalist mode of production prevails, presents itself as an immense accumulation of commodities, its elementary form being a single commodity. Our investigation must therefore begin with the analysis of a commodity"—and its analysis proceeds by taking up definite forms, forms of appearance, forms of value, and more.

Marx often framed his advances beyond existing scholarship in terms of this attention to form. Where bourgeois political economists like Adam Smith and David Ricardo had already described value as produced by labor, Marx departed from their labor theory by contributing an analysis of the different forms value takes on (use-value, exchange-value, surplus value), and of what he always called the "commodity form" as the distinguishing feature of capitalist economies. Early sociologists, industrialists, and activists had all used empirical observation and journalistic techniques to describe the capitalism of the nineteenth century, but Marx added the formalist focus on the systemic nature of capitalism, and on its functioning according to intrinsic principles. Early theorists of money and the credit economy, from Pierre-Joseph Proudhon to Walter Bagehot, had described the predicament of faith and suspense created by the promise of paper money or lines of credit, but Marx added the elaboration of how these apparently subjective experiences constitute the objective system of metaphysics under capitalism, with its orientation toward the future and its deferral of reckoning. In each of these cases, Marx was able to make conceptual innovations because he attended to forms, to systems, to wholes, to composites.

Form is composed relationality. Marx was a thinker of relations, a thinker of and with form, so his critical presuppositions, procedures, and vocabulary lend themselves readily to analysis of forms of cultural production. His signature critical move is to ask why things take the form they do: Why do we have this form of economic production and not another, why do we have this form of class relation and not another? As he described his own analytic project, he aimed "to develop from the actual, given relations of life the *forms* in which these have been apotheosized."[1] He wants to start with observing the empirical, and move from there to the general, to study relations in context in order to abstract to their principles of composition.

In our current university configuration, we probably think of the study of form as a minor subset of soft disciplines like literature, music, and art history. Even in those disciplines, form is often a secondary rather than primary consideration, one among many elements like context, biography, technology that would be introduced in, say, a film studies class. But Marx's work can remind us that form is indispensable for the hard disciplines like economics, sociology, history. Moreover, it can remind us that taking form as a primary object of inquiry rather than a secondary or tertiary topic can actualize an intrinsically Marxian methodology: the study of form can be politically astute and politically consequential. Indeed, prominent Marxist theorists like Georg Lukács, Fredric Jameson, and Sianne Ngai have regarded form as the site of social relationality. In this book I advance this understanding of Marxism as a combination of formalist focus and contextualist rigor, suggesting that Marxism can transcend these shopworn oppositions between soft and hard disciplines, between aesthetics and politics, between formalism and the social.

Germane to Marx's prioritizing of form is his own formal practice. Throughout his career Marx worked in numerous genres, and he was constantly inventing new genres, concerned with the manner of production, circulation, and consumption of ideas about economic and cultural production and the role of representation in those domains. He wrote poetry and plays and a novel; he layered all of his philosophical, political, and journalistic writing with myriad literary and artistic allusions and quotations from an international, transhistorical pantheon of creative writers such as Dante, Cervantes, Shakespeare, Goethe, Balzac, and Dickens. He wrote a manifesto, deftly wielding that genre's reductive and performative features; he wrote stirring expository journalism; and he also wrote painstakingly detailed systematic treatises. He improvised the new genre of "the critique of ideology," starting with his massive and wild 500-page *The German Ideology* (cowritten with Friedrich Engels), a text that sometimes gracefully, sometimes awkwardly incorporates essays, manifestos, declarations of philosophical tenets, logical equations, sustained jokes, lists of maxims, catalogues of uninterpreted quotations, shorthand notes for future elucidation, gnomic slogans, and play-written scripts for the dramas that might take place among his opponents.[2]

Building things with Marxism[3]

Marx's experiments with forms provide just one clue to the importance of form and of building things up for his thought, but this importance itself is key to answering the common charge, from both popular and academic circles, that Marxism is an overly reductive, destructive, and negative endeavor to spoil everything fun and beautiful by exposing the power behind it, and to attack everything normal in the name of dethroning that power. If you bounce around the right-wing cybersphere, or read *The New York Times*, you might think Marxism doesn't want to build anything up—it wants to "destroy," "sabotage," "commit treason," and "wage psychological warfare against America;" in its grips, "western civilization itself is under relentless attack." Ignorance and anti-Semitism underwrite these caricatures, but such rhetoric of Marxism as a force of destruction actually operates very widely, even in more refined spheres. In the academy, to take only the example of cultural studies and literary criticism (let alone political science or economics), the widespread and well-funded movement called "postcritique" faults Marxism for promoting an overly negative view of art, literature, and culture. For example, feminist film theorists celebrate how female spectators find empowerment in films and deplore Marxism as a total bummer. Right-wing fake news and liberal feminist professors surprisingly align.

That spectrum may be united by poor reading, but perhaps Marx set himself up for it, since he described his life's work as "the ruthless critique of everything existing," and the title of the very first work he coauthored with Friedrich Engels was "Critique of Critical Critique." The joke's repetition and tautology betoken Marx's signature ironic tone, the abyssal

downward drive of *judging judging*, the undermining of
everything. This tail-chasing reflexive quality is important:
Kant thought the job of philosophy was to assess itself, to
analyze the subjectivity of the philosopher—and Marx took
this job seriously, noting that the history of philosophy had
not yet reckoned with philosophy's history, had not yet
situated the knowing subject within her historical conditions.
The work of explaining how "the ideas of the ruling class
are in every epoch the ruling ideas" can often seem largely
negative. What is Marxism, but critique of everything existing,
indicting the corruption of everything, exposing the complicity
of even those who want social reform, ever denouncing the
sleeping unwoke? What is critique, but tearing things apart,
revolutionary arson? What is revolution but permanent
revolution, ceaseless churning? What is the critique of critical
critique, but a joke about this hollowness, the chasm of irony
undermining any solid ground on which to stand?

Even in the course of writing his most sustained elaboration
of what materialism is (*The German Ideology*—around the
same time as the *Critique of Critical Critique*), Marx demurred
to define the positive tenets of communism: "Communism
is for us not a state of affairs which is to be established, an
ideal to which reality [will] have to adjust itself. We call
communism the real movement which abolishes the present
state of things." Then just a few years later in *The Manifesto
of the Communist Party*, the genre that is supposed to make
manifest things that have remained unseen, this aura of the
negative remains forefront: as the document concludes "In
short, the communists everywhere support every revolutionary
movement against the existing social and political order of
things. . . . The Communists . . . openly declare that their
ends can be attained only by the forcible overthrow of all
existing social conditions." Marxism's reputation for insatiable
negativity is perhaps not all caricature.

Nor in fact is this reputation always a bad one. In fields
like history, philosophy, and literature, critics who have
claimed Marxism as inspiration—especially the framework

of historical materialism, of studying social life in situ—have often understood their work to be this forcible overthrow—the dismantling of hierarchies, the breaking down of grand narratives, the decomposition of universals. The hallmarks of these enterprises are probably familiar—"Declarations of the universal are problematic." "Rights are a bourgeois construct." "If we invoke the human we bring the baggage of Enlightenment racism." "The state is nothing but an apparatus of violence." Opposing all of these built-up generalities and institutions, theorists understand their work as instead particularizing and taking-apart. Thinking locally, prioritizing "the exceptional, nuanced, situated, concrete, embodied, the historically specific,"[4] critics devote themselves to what eludes classification or massification, what is excluded from formed wholes. For example, the prominent Marxist theorist Jacques Rancière, who claims to devote his work to the liberation of the proletariat, repeatedly argues that politics is the designed configuration of social relations and the corresponding design of sensory experience, and repeatedly associates any such definite configuration, any fixed relations of order, with "the police." The police is any established arrangement for social relation; against it, "the essence of politics consists in disturbing this arrangement," but these disturbances must perpetually disturb themselves—anything sustained or instituted transmutes politics back into the police. Fighting the police, destabilizing order, fueling dissensus, this putatively Marxist project of perpetually overturning anything which stands in place ends up bearing striking resemblance to what Jill Lepore and John Pat Leary have called "the disruption machine," the culture of innovation at the heart of neoliberalism.

In the ecstasy for overturning, for resisting any reification, for spurning institutions, for rejecting constitutions, many political thinkers claiming some allegiance to Marxism have ultimately viewed their work as against constructs and consensus, against synthesis, against building things up. The spectacularly influential political philosopher Giorgio Agamben even has a name for this dissolution and dismantling, which he celebrates as the opposite of constituting: "destituency" (from the Latin *de* + *statuere*—moving away from setting things up, deserting, forsaking, abandoning). Agamben consummates a profound tradition associating constituting and building with violence, and formalization with oppressive containment, and thus for embracing as an alternative unforming, destituting, deconstituting. Agamben names the ethos of formlessness that functions as the ideal uniting a variety of theories and practices, from the mosh of the multitude to the localization of microstruggle and microaggression, from the voluntarist assembly of actors and networks to the flow of affects untethered from the symbolic. Noting its refusal of order, we can call this ideal "anarchovitalism"—the fantasy of life without any built formations, of effusions beyond bounds.

As this ideal has taken hold, it has become a reflex to valorize destituency, taking things apart, and to often claim a Marxist basis for this. But, as we have seen, the elementary lesson of materialism is to situate reflexive positions in their contexts of power—what ruling classes are served by these ruling ideas of demolition? And by contrast, what might be the revolutionary potential of valorizing building? I would argue that Marx's own work actually provides important resources for building. The ruthless critique of everything existing enables making new things. Proactive projection of another order of things is latent in the reactive rejection of this order of things. The work of liberation is the strengthening of those projections into compelling visions, positive platforms, definitive demands, utopian maps.

Marx's norms, Marx's utopian maps

The projective function of Marxism is perceptible in the tacit norms with which Marx frequently frames his materialist constructs. His ideas are designed to serve an active, enabling function in the work for other worlds rather than just for passive documenting of the merely existent world. Even though he invented the practice of ideology critique, exposing how ideas participate in power relations, and even though his radical revisions of materialism set it up as a tool for revealing how norms and normative values uphold unequal distributions of power and wealth, his work also implies that not all norms are bad. After all, his materialism is more than the insight that "ideas" are shaped by context of their production—it is also a great exercise in how ideas exceed context, exceed determination—his materialism is itself an idea! Marx and Engels established critique as an immanent relation to context. Materialism reveals the rootedness of thought in a given society, but it also performs the faculty of thought as uprooting, as pivotal for social transformation. Marxism is the theory and practice of critique of *this* given sociality of capitalism, critique which *this* sociality itself generates, critique which must of necessity be immanent to what exists even while it works for the inexistent, setting out toward utopia.[5]

When the *Manifesto* exhorts the workers of the world to unite, it does so in the interest of implied reversals of the way things are under capitalism. Take a statement like

> In proportion as the bourgeoisie, i.e., capital, is developed, in the same proportion is the proletariat, the modern working class, developed—a class of laborer's, who live only so long as they find work, and who find work only so long as their labor increases capital. These laborer's, who must sell themselves piecemeal, are a commodity, like every other article of commerce, and are consequently exposed to all the vicissitudes of competition, to all the fluctuations of the market.

These lines imply that laborers should be able to live even if they do not find work and should be able to work even if their labor does not increase capital, and should not have to sell themselves piecemeal, like a commodity. The social revolution and the dictatorship of the proletariat Marx and Engels positively call for decisively intervene in the existing world in order to actualize a better world: normatively, things will be better when the regime of surplus value does not organize the production of material life itself, when the norms of the state are to serve the immiserated and expelled.

Creative labor

Perhaps the most essential expression of norms for our film theory purposes is Marx's definition of human beings as creative, constructive *builders*. Rejecting common ways of differentiating human nature from animal nature, Marx settles on the idea that whereas animals merely subsist, humans produce a mode of production: "Men can be distinguished from animals by consciousness, by religion or anything else you like. They themselves begin to distinguish themselves from animals as soon as they begin to produce their means of subsistence, a step which is conditioned by their physical organization." In producing their existence, humans express their essence as productive. Labor exceeds the social relations in which it is ensnared in the capitalist mode of production; it is also a transhistorical faculty of the human. Marx writes,

> Labor is, first of all, a process between man and nature, a process by which man mediates. . . . We understand labor in a form that stamps it as exclusively human. A spider conducts operations that resemble those of a weaver, and a bee puts to shame many an architect in the construction of her cells. But what distinguishes the worst architect from the best of bees is this, that the architect raises his structure in imagination before he erects it in reality. At the end of every labor-process, we get a result that already existed in the imagination of the laborer at its commencement. He not only effects a change of form in the material on which he works, but he also realizes a purpose of his own.[6]

Strikingly, Marx chooses the figure of the architect to emblematize the human—foregrounding the capacity for creative construction. While the bee fulfills needs by changing the form of natural materials, man builds an idea, an imaginative construction, an integral projection of both needs and their fulfillment. Labor is mediation, including the mediation of the material and the ideal. Crucial affinities therefore entwine labor and imaginative representation—which is why Marx complements the figure of the architect with the figure of the poet: "Milton produced *Paradise Lost* in the same way that a silkworm produces silk, as the activation of his own nature." Literary production exemplifies the human's natural productive faculty, its blend of ideal and material making. These tropes of creative construction, of making in the ur-sense of poiesis, powerfully underwrite the Marxian commitment to building.

Artworks are often considered creative rather than productive, something extra on top of real material productivity, something done in the interest of a value that differs from economic value. But Marx's insistence on creativity as an essential component of human labor points to the capacity of creative works to reveal truths about work in general. This revelatory capacity must be central to any Marxist theory of film. Hollywood films are produced for profit, but they are also produced as creative building, projecting fictional worlds, generating new realities.

The emphasis on essential creativity is absolutely central to the Marxist critique of modern society. Animals, Marx points out, create merely to satisfy needs. Humans are animals who have the ability to create for reasons having nothing to do with need, and to bequeath to each other creations for which there is no immediate use. Creative production is the essence of the human; it is this essence which is betrayed or "alienated" by modes of production that make physical survival dependent upon waged compensation for work. "Alienation" in Marxist theory is the name for this estrangement in capitalism: humans are at a distance from their essence as creative producers, they are unwillingly separated from the products of their labor, they are obliged to create specialized pieces of products rather than wholes, they do not reap the full benefits of their efforts. If all humans had food, shelter, and healthcare regardless of whether they earned a wage, they would be freer to keep or dispose of their creations as they liked, and to create things that were not immediately exchangeable or valuable. Workers sell their labor to capitalists; the capitalists in turn own the products of the workers' labor. Workers are thus alienated from, disconnected from, their own products. Owners exacerbate alienation by selling the products of workers' labor and making a profit; workers are distanced from not only their products but also the profits they produce. They further exacerbate alienation by coercing workers to participate in division and specialization in the creative process in order to maximize efficiency.

One of Marx's great contributions to the understanding of human experience is to insist on the ways that what earlier philosophers had described as an existential predicament was actually a contingent, materially conditioned one. It is a feature of the human's essence only insofar as the creative drive tends to result in the externalized creation of objects—whether concrete material goods like tools and crafts or abstract goods like ideas and art—which can then move beyond their creators. But many of the social connotations of alienation—separation from fellow beings, distance from norms of mental health, anxiety about the meaning of life—are not essential so much as the result of specific social processes. The Marxist sense of alienation locates these more diffuse senses within those specific processes, addressing capitalism as a root cause. Marxist theory therefore sometimes suggests that the revolutionary overthrow of capitalism could result in overcoming alienation. Meditations on the status of alienation—including self-division, the division of labor, and social antagonism—may be assessed in terms of whether they project an ultimate identity and integration, or whether they foresee the ongoingness of alienation even after the end of capitalism. We will return to this debate in our analysis of the identity and estrangement problems that preoccupy *Fight Club*.

The intense creativity of human existence is the norm violated by the systematic division of labor and the exploitative conditions of labor, whereby workers are denied the freedom to create heterogeneously.

> In communist society, where nobody has one exclusive sphere of activity but each can become accomplished in any branch he wishes, society regulates the general production and thus makes it possible for me to do one thing today and another tomorrow, to hunt in the morning, fish in the afternoon, rear cattle in the evening, criticize after dinner, just as I have a mind, without ever becoming hunter, fisherman, herdsman or critic. (The German Ideology, p. 53)

The ultimate prescription is for this freedom of creative and life-sustaining activity, a freedom to engage in it as the expression of the species-being, of making and producing and creating, and to engage in it for reasons other than mere survival. This positive vision of expressive existence, of flourishing, Marx does hazard a formula for, very late in his career, in 1875, in another critique—a line-by-line correction to the Gotha Program's statement of positive positions for German socialists—in the course of which he made some positive assertions of his own, some of the most forthright statements of his own convictions:

> In a higher phase of communist society, after the enslaving subordination of the individual to the division of labor, and therewith also the antithesis between mental and physical labor, has vanished; after labor has become not only a means of life but life's prime want; after the productive forces have also increased with the all-around development of the individual, and all the springs of co-operative wealth flow more abundantly—only then then can the narrow horizon of bourgeois right be crossed in its entirety and society inscribe on its banners: From each according to his ability, to each according to his needs![7]

The fulcrum of this formula is the unstable asymmetry of ability and needs, either side always incommensurate with its other.

This incommensurability gives the lie to any wish for a simple, flowing, social immanence. More just states must be highly designed formations, avowing their merely formal character, offering themselves for constant reform and rebuilding as asymmetries and antagonisms irrupt. This formal problematic is encoded in Marx's most allusive, most direct position on the state: the dictatorship of the proletariat. What Marx means by this apparent paradox—how can you take the masses and make them singular as a dictator?—is that we must find a political formation that supports contradictions, that admits its own contradictory quality.

Contradictions in motion—not synthesis but the negation of the negation which radically produces a something that is not nothing—these ideas in Marx's rare writings on the state position the state not as ends but as means—a technique of flourishing, a variform base. His point is never that there should be no organized institutions of social life, but rather that those institutions should be infrastructures in the service of social life. His writings on the Paris Commune affirm "the reabsorption of the state power by society as its own living forces instead of as forces controlling and subduing it, by the popular masses themselves, forming their own force instead of the organized force of their oppression," and he works with similar images of absorption and skeletal support in concluding "Freedom consists in converting the state from an organ superimposed upon society into one completely subordinate to it." These commitments to organization, to the party, to reabsorbed state power, to the subordinate organ of the state, to infrastructure distinguish Marx's thought as a program invested in composed relations and in new energies of composition, of building things up.

Perhaps, then, what Marxism builds in the world is a willingness to think about definite forms of relationality as the spaces of existence—rather than to think about form as police, as order that must be anarchically abolished, as an obstacle to a formlessness fantasized as freedom. What Marxism builds is a practice of thinking infrastructurally, risking dialectical regard for forms, reaching for spaces more adequate for human beings (to invoke Ernst Bloch's definition of utopia). Critique, like hunting and fishing and cattle rearing, is an essential human activity for Marx, an expression of the creative faculty that is the always laboring, always making being. The ruthless overturning of everything existing finds its dialectical complement in the dynamic making of new existences, new things, new forms, new orders. We practice this making not in the maker-culture of entrepreneur tech and industrial engineering, but in humanities endeavors of imaginative projection, enabling abstraction, compelling storytelling, creative synthesis, and the choreography of solidarity. The study of forms is more than just destruction—it is the affirmation of composed relationality, formedness rather than formlessness, that we may better pursue the arts of social building.

Marx built his philosophy by seeing form in the world and by proffering concepts that could help others see as well. Three of the key concepts in his thought will anchor the rest of our discussion: mode of production, ideology, and mediation. We will explore these concepts in his thought and in Marxist theory after him, and then we will also turn, in Chapter 2, to how these concepts are elaborated by *Fight Club*.

Mode of production

In his project of analyzing forms, critiquing forms, and advocating for new forms, Marx invented a number of constructs that are aimed at making perceptible the forms of relationality, the frameworks of organization, that comprise the infrastructures of the social. These constructs are abstractions of these definite forms, meant to reveal the role of form in history. For example, he proposed the major concept of "the mode of production" to convey the idea that the activity of producing and reproducing collective existence has no natural form, but rather takes many contingent forms throughout history. "Mode of production" (*produktionsweise*) is the way life itself is produced: as he introduces it, "life involves before everything else eating and drinking, a habitation, clothing, and many other things. The first historical act is thus the production of the means to satisfy these needs, the production of material life itself." This production of material life consists of two levels in combination. These are the *forces* of production (resources, labor, technology, materials, land) and the *relations* of production (the social and political relationships among the people whose material lives are being produced—relations such as associations, class, property, law, power). What results from the mode of production is a *totality*—an ensemble for organizing the whole of existence, and for reproducing that constellation of relations into the future, that is marked by its contingency, its incompletion, its possibility of being otherwise. Totality is not "all the things"— it is the contradiction between a specific situation and other possibilities, and the principal of thinking this contradiction at this level.

When Marx first introduces the concept of mode of production, in his preface to his *Contribution to the Critique of Political Economy*, he writes "The mode of production in material life determines the general character of the social, political, and spiritual processes of life." Mode of production is a concept then that doesn't just encompass economic relations, but also addresses how economic relations are a "determining" factor in other kinds of relations. Because economics is at its root the organization of the conditions for human survival ("economy" from the Greek *nomos*, meaning law, and *oikos*, meaning *house* or *hearth*), every society will have some sort of economy. Marxism in turn is the approach to human history and human relations which insists that whatever sort of economy is in place will be determining for the kinds of culture that will be in place—the kinds of social relations, the kinds of political organizations, the kinds of everyday practices, and the kinds of beliefs. "Determining" is thus a crucial dynamic in the Marxist way of thinking. In the simplest terms, determination for Marx means limits on what will happen, but it does not mean prescriptions of what will happen. He writes: "In all forms of society it is a determinate production and its relations which assigns every other production and its relations their rank and influence. It is a general illumination in which all other colors are plunged, and which modifies their specific tonalities. It is a special ether which defines the specific gravity of everything found within it."[8] These images of light influencing the tone of color or air effecting the factors of gravity are instructive as natural metaphors; for Marx it would seem that the relationship of determination is natural. Marxism prioritizes the collective production of conditions of collective household life ("eating and drinking, a habitation, clothing") as an inevitable natural occurrence that, however contingent its shape, exercises a natural influence over what gets shaped.

Determination means that economic relations are foundational, and that the contingent type of economic relations sets some limits upon the variety of social, political, and spiritual relations that attend any given mode of production. To clarify that these limits are structuring but not controlling, that they configure possibilities but do not foreclose all possibility, the Marxist theorist Louis Althusser invoked the concept of "overdetermination." He borrowed the concept from Sigmund Freud, who seems to have coined it himself. In *Studies on Hysteria*, Freud uses "overdetermined" (*uberdeterminiert*) to insist that hysteria has multiple causes that are social and psychological, not merely physiological. Similarly, in *The Interpretation of Dreams*, he sets out to overcome the entrenched orthodoxy that dreams are allegories, writing "there are no limits to the determinants that may be present" and he interestingly makes recourse to an industrial analogy: "Here we find ourselves in a factory of thought where, as in the Weaver's masterpiece, 'a thousand threads one treadle throws, where fly the shuttles over here, over there' . . . each of the elements of the dream's content turns out to have been overdetermined—to have been represented in the dream-thoughts many times over."[9] Freud's concept names a factory of causes, all busy, weaving together the fabric of what happens. When Althusser takes up this notion, it has this connotation of busy, concerted production that amounts to a state of things which is itself irreducible to any factor in the busy-ness. Overdetermination for Althusser indicates limits, or "causes," that exceed any effect; there are too many causes for an effect to be said to issue directly. The concept also indicates for Althusser the meeting ground between what he calls "a historical inhibition" and that of "revolutionary rupture": at every moment that a particular mode of production continues to operate, it is holding off a revolutionary rupture, inhibiting a flow of history. Overdetermination is this engineered suspense, the continued effectivity of the present order of things.

The mode of production determines culture—not in the sense of causing it, but in the sense of providing too many causes for it. Althusser thus also arrives at another famous formula: political, social, cultural, and spiritual relations enjoy a "relative autonomy" from the economy. Insofar as they are limited, but not prescribed, or caused but not reductively caused, these dynamics are partially contingent, independent from the mode of production. This independence can be understood temporally: culture can outlast the mode of production, and it can anticipate new modes of production. But it can also be understood logically: culture can reproduce the status quo, while it can also critique the status quo and performatively bring about some other status. Either way, it must be understood dialectically—hence the adverb "relatively," which is a qualifier just like the "over" in "overdetermination." To analyze culture and cultural productions like film requires attending to both overdetermination and relative autonomy, to both reproducing the way things are and precipitating something else.

In the course of setting out his definition of the mode of production, Marx employs a metaphor that continues to be vividly used and hotly debated. In the same passage from the preface to the *Contribution to the Critique of Political Economy* we were already examining, he continues:

> In the social production which men carry on they enter into definition relations that are indispensable and independent of their will; these relations of production correspond to a definite stage of development of their material powers of production. The sum total of these relations of production constitutes the economic structure of society—the real basis on which rise legal and political superstructures, and to which correspond the definite forms of social consciousness.[10]

This architectural metaphor of a foundation and super-structure (*basis* and *uberbau*) is one of the most enduring legacies of Marxian materialism.

This metaphor works to provide a model for understanding the interdependent infrastructure of social formations. It illustrates that what has been built up as social existence has different components that are structurally integrated. The basis supports and enables what stands upon it. Materialism addresses this base and this relation of support or correspondence. But the model doesn't say what it means to correspond; it doesn't say that correspondence between base and superstructure, economic structure and social consciousness, is totalizing. Similarly, Marx explains that "it is not the consciousness of men that determines their existence, but their social existence that determines their consciousness." Yet Marx's own ideas, the whole superstructure of values and methods and norms and insights which he generates to be intensely critical of the capitalist mode of production, "rise" atop that mode, and "correspond" to it.

The "Mode of Production" is a construct that renders available the constructions of sociality and brings into relief the possibility of other such constructions. Capitalism is only one mode of production; but all socialities can be fathomed as productive, as activated by the production of material life itself, comprised of both forces and relations. The goal of transforming capitalism isn't ending production, but ending this particularly unjust mode, and arranging the mode differently. That is the force of Marx's use of "mode" (or "way" in German): capitalism is one way of producing, and naming this way helps us cognize us other ways. History provides examples of other ways, and what progress there is in history prompts the reckoning that there may be as yet unactualized ways in the future. If the normative goal of Marxist theorizing is greater freedom for laborers, the very idea of "the capitalist mode of production" points toward the possibility of a mode with a different adjective, perhaps the communist mode of production, perhaps the humanist mode of production, perhaps the contingent mode of production.

To enrich our understanding of other possibilities, Marx conducts studies of historical examples, and projects future options. History features examples of tribalism, feudalism, capitalism. The future, yet to be historically instantiated, may include socialism and communism. In many ways Marx implies that human world history is moving along a trajectory, a progression through stages of different modes, and a progression with a tendency toward increasing human freedom. The capitalist mode can therefore look like a midway point between the principled inequality of the past and the concrete equality to come.

The tribal mode of production obtains before the agricultural revolution and encompasses hunter-gatherers and nomadic peoples. Anthropological and archaeological evidence points to such a social organization, revealing a priority of kinship relations. Although Marx and Engels refer to class struggle as present throughout history, the tribal modes may have been sufficiently small as to rely more upon kinship hierarchies than economic classes. Sometimes Marx and Engels attribute to this era of human history a possible configuration they call "primitive communism," an egalitarian and cooperative mode in which production occurs for collective use rather than for commodity exchange, but since they based these ideas on eighteenth- and nineteenth-century archaeological thinkers like Bachofen and Morgan, a certain imperial tint comes with the concept. Imagining non-Western territories as non-capitalist could provide justification for the allegedly civilizing mission of colonialism and imperialism. Even with these pitfalls, however, the concept of the tribal mode of production holds open the prehistory of capitalism, outlining a way in which human beings produced their own means of existence without the instrument of private property.

In feudalism, an expansive period of human history, the majority of peoples subsist as slaves and peasants, in loose social organizations that nonetheless redound to rigid hierarchies, empowering a small minority to control land and resources, often through violence, threats of starvation, and physical force. Most resources are held privately, with little function of a political institution like the state to regulate publicly held resources. Feudalism involves an open acknowledgment of inequality, in turn rationalized as natural, divinely ordained, and/or otherwise meritoriously apportioned. The feudal mode of production allocates glory and wealth and health to the limited few, and fear and endurance to the rest. This mode of production uses violence to hold itself in place and unlike capitalism, it does not in any way obscure its real conditions of existence. Peasants lack a right to private property, and slaves lack any rights at all. Feudal lords can engage in parallel relations with other lords through trade, conquest, and war; the feudal system takes its name from the Latin *feudum* meaning fief, domains that lords and emperors award to vassals in exchange for their military service or war/trade counsel. Over time, multiple empires and kingdoms—Carolingian, Ottoman, English, and Anglo-Norman—developed, entailing the growth of cities like Venice and London, of mercantile technologies, and of market relations. Urbanization and trade are crucial components of capitalism, but the feudal period differs from capitalism because the impetus of these institutions is the *use* of goods by the feudal class, in lavish displays of wealth—not accumulation for accumulation's sake. In the twenty-first century, some scholars have begun to speak of "refeudalization" as dramatically rising inequality, regimes of austere scarcity and of severe debt, insidious privatization of formerly public resources, the moralization of wealth, and criminalization of poverty have pitched late capitalism back toward feudal relations.

Capitalism transforms feudal use into aristocratic/bourgeois accumulation, and peasant/slave subsistence into working class exploitation. One element of this transformation is "enclosure," the full privatization of lands upon which peasants had subsisted without owning, and the consequent expulsion of peasants onto a market in which rather than toil for their survival in largely agricultural fashion, they sold their labor for wages in mercantile and industrial fashion. The invention of financial technologies like credit, stock, and insurance in the early modern period fueled the basic principle of this mode of production, the accumulation of surplus value. Another indispensable element of the transformation is the informal and formal abolition of the slave relation (especially through the Haitian Revolution and the policies of the British Empire), since capitalism apotheosizes abstract freedom, the freedom of all to sell themselves. Capitalism promises freedom: peasants liberated from the land, lords liberated from obligations to their vassals and serfs, workers liberated by machines, social relations liberated from fixed hierarchies of blood and tradition, opened to the floods of profit and professionals.

Marx was keenly attuned to this promise, pointing to the contradiction between its abstract message and its concrete realities. Freed from subsistence farming on de facto public land, peasants found themselves starving and anonymous in overcrowded cities, reeling from unregulated conditions in dangerous factories. Why should surplus accumulation be the principle determining how human beings organize the production of their own existence? Why not collective flourishing and the common? In asking these questions, Marx pointed toward concrete freedoms. To hunt in the morning, fish in the afternoon, rear cattle in the evening, criticize after dinner; from each according to his ability, to each according to his needs. The communist mode of production would marshal capitalist technological advancement in the service of communal well-being, disarticulating human productive activity from the wage relation, disarticulating human survival from selling labor. Communism is ultimately nothing for Marx other than this concrete practice of freedom to make and to live, freedom to transform social relations, to evolve the mode of production, to participate in the open future of "the real movement to abolish the present state of things."

The concept of "the mode of production" demarcates the past from the present and the future, and underscores that those differences are not inevitable or natural, but the result of deliberate human activity. The idea that a few thousand years of human history could be meaningfully apprehended in a schema of a few categories may strike some as overly grand and overly reductive. The Marxist effort to articulate these varying modes of production points therefore to tensions between what we now understand as the disciplinary protocols of history and those of philosophy. What is so important and useful about such a philosophical rendering of history is the way it issues from a political conjuncture and a political vision: Marx and Engels want to relativize the capitalist mode of production— to reveal that it is the result of specific historical events and configurations, and to reveal that it is not the only possible way to organize human existence. Their schema accomplishes this by giving names to other principles of organization without private property, or without abstract freedom.

Mode of reproduction

The concept of the mode of production aims at relativizing individual modes, thinking about their particulars so that they don't appear as natural or as the only possibilities.

An entailed concept is that any given mode of production must include derelativizing—must hold itself in place, keep itself going, sustain the relations that enable it. The Marxist name for this dynamic is "reproduction." The "re" captures the element of repetition, since supporting a system is ensuring its ongoingness, its repeatability. But the "re" also captures two other colloquial senses of origination: (1) Going back to the starting point/bringing something into existence again/sexual reproduction, and (2) Copying/simulating/producing a text, image, or idea again. Marx writes "every social process of production is, at the same time, a process of reproduction" and Althusser elaborated the function of ideology in perpetuating the capitalist mode of production in an essay called "On the Reproduction of Capitalism."[11] Reproduction brings the mode of production back to its origins—every society will produce, will have an economy. It also brings the mode of production into relief as a strategy of copying, producing itself over and over.

Like the concept of the mode of production, the concept of social reproduction helps clarify that Marxism is not just focused on economics, is not simply an analysis of economic systems, but is a synoptic view of the diverse social practices and social relations that constitute capitalism. Part of the configuration of the forces and relations of production in the capitalist mode is the perpetuation of that mode. The problem of social reproduction raises the question "Who produces the worker who produces?" Feminist theorists have thus been particularly interested in this concept, since it points to the unofficial, unwaged labor of generating and sustaining labor, or to the off-the-books costs of socially enabling human existence. When Marx defined labor as making, and as the key feature of all of human history, he opened the door to thinking about the labor that goes in to making human society, into raising workers who then sell their labor when they are older.

Understandings of this labor, in scholarship by Silvia Federici, Nancy Fraser, Tithi Battacharya, and others, return to the roots of "economy," the law of the house, since labor that is not part of the wage relation is nonetheless part of the mode of production. Specifically, women are often laboring to bear pregnancies, nurse infants, tend toddlers, and raise independent children, as well as care for elders, while also laboring to cook, clean, and maintain a household—yet none of this labor is directly compensated by the owners of the means of production. The capitalist mode of production reproduces itself by means of unwaged labor that brings workers into existence, an origin for human beings that isn't reducible to capitalism. When women are able to work outside of the home for a wage, they generally then employ women lower on the social scale than themselves to substitute for this labor, such as young women, old women, immigrant women, non-white women. The subordination and exploitation of women, including the subordination and exploitation of women of color, is therefore built into the capitalist mode of production, since the powerful forces and relations of production include the power to value and devalue labor. The concept of social reproduction helps illustrate that there are other possible modes of production because it marks the difference between the work it takes to make the human animal capable of work and the goal of surplus accumulation. We undertake the work of producing existence for reasons other than surplus accumulation. And this would be true even if all domestic work was wage work. The survival of the species is an end that differs from capitalist ends. So are love, pleasure, and community.

One of the tricks of the capitalist mode is to try to incorporate these alternatives, these other ends of action, into itself. Thus the "love" parents might spontaneously feel for their offspring becomes a vehicle for upholding the wage theft the capitalist effectively commits in not compensating its workers for the costs of the sustenance of their emergence as workers, since parents are told it is "meaningful" to give up wage work or careers when a child is born to stay home. Defining words like love and meaning and wage, and the everyday practices those definitions enable, thus become a material force for the mode of production.

For some feminists, the historical fact that patriarchy predates the systematic transition to the capitalist mode of production contradicts the analytic power of Marxism, since it will never, they claim, be able to account for axes of social relations that exceed capitalism. This charge is also sometimes levied by theorists of race, though the historical facts of precedence are more contested there, since many historians and theorists argue that the emergence of race as an epistemological and social category tracks closely with the consolidation of capitalism. But some of the strength of Social Reproduction Theory, as it is now called by contemporary Marxist feminists, is to point out repeatedly that what look like independent kinds of social relations ancillary to capitalism are actually integral to its normal functioning in everyday life and its historical trajectory through dynamics like primitive accumulation and the expulsion of surplus populations. We don't know what societies and modes of production look like that don't rely on gendering and racialization, but that doesn't invalidate the quest to devise a different mode of production.

In addition to the material support for capitalism that gendered and racialized persons provide, sexism and racism provide support as ideas. They are frameworks of meaning that make capitalist domination and exploitation appear justified, that make the capitalist mode of production seem like the only one. These meanings become a material force for the mode of production. This notion of an immaterial material force is our second key word.

Ideology

How can a mode of production and its attendant social relations be perceived? From what vantage? What holds the capitalist mode of production in place? What is the epoxy that can withstand the pull of profound social contradictions? Why do we participate in our own exploitation? What is the connection between the economic production of goods and the artistic, philosophical, and religious articulation of the good? The Marxist notion of ideology outlines these questions. Trying to answer them has kept theorists busy for generations. My discussion below moves through several moments of this theorizing in largely chronological order, although the intent is not to imply that more recent theories of ideology are more correct. As we will see eventually in the analysis of ideology in *Fight Club* in Chapter 2, each of these theories can helpfully shed light on different aspects of social relations and the consciousness of those relations.

In our colloquial usages, and even in many misconceived theories, "ideology" means a scheme for politics, a set of committed beliefs about what should be done in society. If you understand the term this way, then you can speak of "Marx's ideology" or "Marxist ideology" as the critique of the capitalist mode of production and the advocacy for a more collective, more emancipatory mode. But Marx not only had an ideology, he also spent a lot of energy theorizing what ideology is.

His theorizing refined the work of earlier philosophers. For eighteenth-century thinkers, "ideology" meant rather literally "the science of ideas," and referred chiefly to the enterprise of knowing how we know. The implied contrast was between ideology and metaphysics, where metaphysics would maintain that ideas existed in some real sense and then living thinkers accessed them, and ideology would be the more empirical study of how ideas only exist among specific thinkers (i.e., among humans). In the eighteenth century, ideology signified precisely this empirical study, the "science of ideas," and is associated with Enlightenment thinkers like DeStutt de Tracy. The term acquired the pejorative sense often associated with it—an agenda, a bias—after the French Revolution, when Napoleon himself derided the republicanism of philosophers that seemed to contest his power by calling them "ideologues," proponents of "that shadowy metaphysics which subtly searches for first causes on which to base the legislation of peoples, rather than making use of laws known to the human heart and the lessons of history."[12] For Napoleon, ideologists were those interested in liberal principles of rationalizing law and exploring consent rather than those who simply naturalized the current order of things. They were needlessly partisan, taking exception to nature.

Marx departed from both the quasi-science and the philosophies of liberalism by developing a theory of ideology rooted in the question of the social relations from within which any science of ideas or any debate about republican sovereignty could be undertaken. He insisted on the social dimension of the activity of specific thinkers, on their social location and on their participation in the configuration of power in their context. For him the previous accounts of ideology had been too immaterial, too focused on intellectual abstractions. By way of correction, he wanted to underline the material relations and practices that give rise to ideas. But the way practices give rise to ideas is not predetermined—ideas may describe practices (as the idea of materialism does), may reflect practices in some partial or distorted way, or may obscure practices. The importance of this range of possibilities is that there is not a one-to-one correspondence between ideas and practices. There is instead a rift or gap: "Individuals . . . may appear (*erscheinen*) in their own or other people's representation (*Vorstellung*)" different from how "they really (*wirklich*) are; i.e. as they operate (*wirken*), produce materially, and hence as they work under definite material limits, presuppositions and conditions independent of their will." This gap between representations and operations, between how we produce ideally and how we produce materially, has to be studied in its particulars; materialism is that study. It becomes necessary to analyze particular ideas in relation to material practices in order to understand what representational form they take. There can be no ideas outside of material relations of existence, and since those relations always take contingent shape, ideas—even those that claim to be universal or eternal—will always be marked by contingency. "Consciousness can never be anything else than conscious existence, and the existence of men is their actual life-process." From the name of the study of ideas, ideology shifts for Marx to be the name of the contingency of ideas, since there cannot be an objective study.

To elaborate this notion of the contingency and positionality of ideas, Marx early on invoked the architectural metaphor of the base and superstructure that we have already encountered. Through this metaphor, we can say that for Marx ideology is superstructure, the ideas that correspond to the mode of production. The capitalist mode of production determines consciousness under capitalism, and that determined consciousness is ideology. These dialectical relations of correspondence and determination point to Marx's interest in ideology as the general name of the interpenetration of material relations and their ideal counterparts. This interpenetration is true for any mode of production, and configuring it differently is one of the tasks of revolutionary social change. Marx writes:

A distinction should always be made between the material transformation of the economic conditions of production, which can be determined with the precision of natural science, and the legal, political, religious, aesthetic, or philosophic—in short, ideological—forms in which men become conscious of this conflict and fight it out.[13]

Here Marx indicates that ideology is a political idea not just designating agendas or standpoints, nor even designating the political context for ideas as he himself laid out, but also designating entire systems of ideas and representations and practices encompassing the law and courts, spirituality and churches, philosophy and wisdom, art and literature. Moreover, ideology is a way of becoming conscious of social contradiction, which suggests that it is a representation of contradictions that can have multiple uses. The representation might be inaccurate or false; it might be accurate and critical; it is likely some of both. Ideology is ambivalent, a way of becoming conscious of social contradictions which can simultaneously generate recognition of those contradictions and propound misrecognition of them.

Ideology and the camera

In addition to the superstructure metaphor, Marx's own theory of ideology crafts another analogy that will be very consequential for our discussion of film studies. The inevitability of ideology and impossibility of objectivity/necessity for situated knowing, for the material practice of interpretation, compels Marx to make an analogy between ideology and the physical reality of the human eye. There is no way to see that isn't ideological; ideology is a complicated natural process: "If in all ideology men and their relations appear upside-down as in a *camera obscura*, this phenomenon arises just as much from their historical life process as the inversion of objects on the retina does from their physical life-process."[14] Ideology is the production of images through physical processes like vision and the functioning of the optic nerve. Strikingly, the analogy transpires by way of a technology of perception, the camera obscura. From Latin for "dark room," a camera obscura is small box that channels light rays though pinholes within the interior of the box to project images of the setting exterior to the box. The images of the exterior appear in the interior in inverted form. Even though the image is inverted, it preserves dimension, ratio, and color. Human vision works in the same way, since the pupil is a pinhole through which exterior settings are refracted inside the dark space of the eye. There is no way to see without inversion.

Significantly for our purposes in this book, Marx makes this analogy between vision, technology, and ideology in 1845, a mere year after the main inventor of photography, William Henry Fox Talbot, published the first ever book of photography. The historical coincidence between the theory of ideology and the technology of photography suggest the intimate connection between the two. It is hard to theorize ideology, the way that illusions exert material power, without recourse to the camera, the material production of illusion. Marx's reference to the camera obscura goes so far as to argue that there is no way to see other than through the inversions on the retina; there is no way to gain access to the world without the filter of representation. When we look at the world, we are looking from a particular vantage, but we are also looking at phenomena that have developed through historical processes that are not merely natural evolutions. We see in bias, and we see bias. Philosophers are not objective describers of a neutral terrain but interested participants in a social field.

The German Ideology, the work in which Marx and Engels introduce their notion of ideology and explain how materialism enables the critique of ideology, is anchored by this sense of the unseen, unacknowledged political investments of philosophy in their day. The dominant thinkers of their time, received as expositors of a universal human condition, were, Marx and Engels pointed out, predominantly Christian, and thus enjoying clout because of their consistency with the power structure of the church in Germany. "It has not occurred to any one of these philosophers to inquire into the connection of German philosophy with German reality," they wrote of popular thinkers. If they were to inquire, they would find that "the ideas of the ruling class are in every epoch the ruling ideas; i.e., the class which is the ruling material force of society, is at the same time its ruling intellectual force." Marx and Engels thus encouraged approaching philosophy as a practice that participated in the production and reproduction of reality. Ideas are in this view not a mechanical reflection of their context but an active agent in creating context.

Because ideology is seeing, a representation of a reality that is itself a projected coherence atop material practices, it is everywhere, inevitable, and constitutive of both obfuscation and critical illumination. When we are deluded about material practices—convinced, say, that the capitalist mode of production is the only one, or is natural—we are seeing ideologically, but when we are arguing that there are other modes of production possible, that this one is unjust and unnecessary, we are also seeing ideologically. Analyzing this agency of ideas within their own reality is, very importantly, not defined by Marx as some kind of throwing back the veil and exposing who is ideological and who isn't. The opposite of ideology isn't getting free of ideology; it is rather the ongoing interpretation of the context of ideas. Marx sets out a procedure that is seemingly unending, and he calls this ongoing interpretation "the *writing* of history." It takes narrative and perspective and duration to be able to fathom ideology.

The falsity of "false consciousness"

In theories of ideology after Marx, there is an unfortunate tendency to forget this ongoingness of the writing of history and to forget this impossibility of seeing without ideology. Too often, ideology has been defined as "false consciousness." The phrase itself comes from a private letter written by Engels, a decade after Marx's death, in which he writes "Ideology is a process accomplished by the so-called thinker consciously, it is true, but with a false consciousness. The real motive forces impelling him remain unknown to him; otherwise it simply would not be an ideological process. Hence he imagines false or seeming motive forces." Engels didn't intend this letter for publication, but the notion that people act without understanding their own motives eventually travelled widely into much political and philosophical discourse and became embellished to include the claim that this lack of understanding could be seen not just as ignorance (or unconsciousness) but as a distorted or wrong kind of consciousness. Georg Lukács picked up the term in the 1920s in his famous work *History and Class Consciousness* to explain why not every member of the working class espouses revolutionary understanding of their contradictory relationship to the ruling class. He had read Engels's letter and suggested the phrase "false consciousness" as a description of the state of mind in which most men conduct their everyday deeds. Urging a dialectical approach, Lukács did not recommend contrasting false consciousness with "true" consciousness, but rather "investigat[ing] this false consciousness concretely as an aspect of the historical totality." The implied other of ideology is therefore not "non-ideology" nor "truth" but "investigating," studying, contextualizing, and "the writing of history."

Despite Lukács's caution, the allure of the idea of false consciousness proved too strong, and many theorists have fallen for it. Herbert Marcuse was one source of its continued circulation, since his 1964 book *One-Dimensional Man* offered extremely catchy analysis of the "false needs" that consumer society engenders and the "false consciousness" that reproduces "a false order of facts."[15] Marcuse's book was reviewed in the popular press, and he was the undergrad and masters advisor for the incredibly influential scholar-activist Angela Davis. "False consciousness" became a very handy phrase for describing the 1960s project of "consciousness raising," and it continues to be a prevailing colloquial meaning of "ideology."

As other Marxist theories emerged, the problematic of false consciousness endured. Antonio Gramsci incorporates false consciousness into his notion of "common sense," part of his argument that the theory of ideology needs to be supplemented by a construct of "hegemony." Hegemony means rule, and Gramsci differentiates between rule by force and rule by ideas. Hegemony therefore functions like a synonym for ideology which circumvents some of the pitfalls of consciousness since it refers to the system of rule rather than something like mind-sets. Hegemony especially captures the power of ideology to hold the capitalist mode of production in place even when economic conditions are ripe for, or indeed enable, a proletarian revolution. Why do revolts and revolutions take place only to fail, falling back into capitalism? Hegemony answers why, since it names ideology as the entrenched system of values, ideas, and beliefs that can resecure the economic regime of private property and surplus extraction even after workers revolt against that regime. For him, "beliefs and ideas are themselves material forces," and thus class conflict can and must take place not only in the material economic arena (i.e., in strikes, riots, occupations) but also in a war of ideas.[16]

False consciousness is a very weak way to theorize ideology. As diluted versions of Lukács, Marcuse, and Gramsci have flowed into academic inquiry and criticism, false consciousness has reigned as an easy umbrella term for why things are the way they are, why intellectuals are important, and why the global revolutionary energy of the 1960s and early 1970s dissipated into the retrenched capitalism of the neoliberal era. The problem with the rubric of false consciousness is that it implies the existence of true consciousness. It thus imagines an outside of ideology, an authoritative or enlightened position from which to critique the false. But the whole point of the Marxist theory of ideology is that all ideas are situated. We are being the most ideological precisely when we feign to be outside, since our outside-ness is still a part of the matrix of social practices that give rise to ideas. Moreover, the notion of false consciousness cannot account for the ways that the capitalist mode of production reproduces itself without regard for our beliefs. It doesn't matter what we think; it matters what we do. As Marx himself put it, "They do not know it, but they are doing it."

Doing not believing

The most decisive theory of ideology as what we do comes from Louis Althusser in his essay "Ideology and Ideological State Apparatuses." His major insight is that ideology is not the beliefs that attach individuals to a particular mode of production, but the everyday habits, rituals, behaviors, and processes that keep the system going. There is thus no such thing as a society without ideology. Base and superstructure exist in all societies; ideology, as he put it, "has no history." But there are different kinds of superstructures, and Althusser distinguishes at least two: the *repressive state apparatus* (RSA) which keeps things going through violence (the police, the military, what we now call the prison industrial complex, etc.) and the *ideological state apparatus* (ISA) which keeps things going through everyday life (family, religion, education, media, recreation). Aside from the question of violence, the two apparatuses differ in that the repressive is relatively unified (agencies working together for law and order, on threat of prison and death) and the ideological is relatively plural (disparate institutions and industries with potentially conflictual goals, and divergent techniques for upholding law and order). The capitalist mode of production mobilizes both apparatuses, but may be understood to break with the historically preceding feudal mode of production by placing relatively less weight on the repressive apparatus: whereas a monarchy enforces its authority through ultimate violence like execution or war on the whim of the king, capitalism relies more upon the practices that are at once freely conducted (which church to go to, how much school, what newspaper to read, whether to get married) and simultaneously indispensable to propagating the general matrix of social practices. It is the material practice that secures our reality. It doesn't matter how little we believe in capitalism's truth, or how snarkily we analyze its limitations—it matters that we live our lives all day within it, keeping it going. Ideology is not our consciousness; it is our actions. To illustrate this, Althusser draws upon Pascal's scandalous formula of religion: "Kneel down, move your lips in prayer, and you shall believe."

To show the efficacy of the beliefs our actions create, Althusser employs the notion of "interpellation," the process by which the ideological state apparatus calls a concrete individual into being as a subject—that is, as a recognized agent with capacities and desires. Famously Althusser illustrates interpellation in a scenario: a person is walking down the street, noticing a police officer but going about her own business. After passing the police officer, hears someone yell "Hey, You!," and she responds by turning around, looking toward the officer. In this scenario, the person has imagined that she is being spoken to, imagined that the speaker is the police officer, and felt an obligation to respond. Admittedly, Althusser's example is confusing, since he is using an interaction with the RSA to illustrate his idea of the ISA. But the example nonetheless dramatizes the gap that interests Althusser, the gap between the embodied person walking down the street, and the interpellated subject that imagines itself being recognized. This gap is elaborated in the work of Jacques Lacan, the structuralist psychoanalyst who emphasized the role of language in constituting the psyche. We are spoken to before we can speak; we are subjected to the (m)other's ideas of us before we can act; we do not choose our own names or social position at birth—and all of these external social factors contribute to forming our internal life. In borrowing this framework, Althusser thereby suggests that even our psychology is its own ideological state apparatus, propagating a sense of identity and of being recognized that ultimately shores up the social system which grants the identity. Even what we think of as our private cores are always already public, and thus conditioned by the contingent mode of production into which we are born.

Althusser's theory of ideological state apparatuses rests on an understanding that the practices and interpellations promoted by institutions cultivate an imaginary vision of what society is. Even though ISAs are not unified in their content or form, they may ultimately converge in projecting a reality which individuals find coherent and which is itself a representation of the mode of production, or what Althusser calls "the real conditions of existence." As we have seen, the capitalist mode of production is a configuration of the conditions of existence for the sake of extracting value from the mass of human beings and amassing that value as wealth in the hands of the few. The capitalist ISA represents that configuration as if it were for the sake of freedom and optimization. An imaginary relationship to real conditions of existence prevails. Ideology is not that imaginary relationship directly; it is rather, and this is Althusser's crucial point, the *representation* of that imaginary relationship. "What is represented in ideology is not the system of the real relations which govern the existence of individuals, but the imaginary relation of those individuals to the real relations in which they live." Ideology within the apparatus is practices (going to school). Ideology within the mind of the practicing individuals is the meaning created that articulates imaginary relations. For example, we tell ourselves that we go to school to get an education, to learn about the world, to become more well-rounded people. But in many ways schooling exists to reproduce the compliant labor force for the capitalist mode of production. Ideology is the *practice* of going to school, and it is the *representation* of going to school as if it is meaningful for reasons other than social reproduction.

The contrast between real conditions and the representation of an imaginary relationship to them mobilizes another of Lacan's ideas, his schema of the real, the imaginary, and the symbolic. Lacan invokes these three registers to organize his study of mental and social life. The imaginary is the realm of images and projections, of identifications and fantasies, of wholes and connections. The symbolic is the realm of language and order, of social norms, customs, habits, rules, laws, and our ability to represent them. The real is the realm of what eludes symbolization, either because it is what any particular social order must exclude to generate its own consistency or because it is something prior to the mediations of the imaginary and the symbolic (i.e., something material, something impossible, something like the disturbance in nature which produces the universe and is embodied in human drive).

For his formula of the opposition between the imaginary and the real, Althusser activates Lacan's theory of registers: the imaginary is fundamentally a realm of the image, whereas the real resists representation (as image and as symbol). The imaginary makes up our reality while the real is the material support of that reality which does not appear within it. To put this back into the Marxist terms we are starting to use, the real could be thought of as unformed nature including the human animal, whereas the imaginary is the specific mode of production through which human animals are able to exist and through which they transform nature. But this translation also shows how slippery the fusion of Marxism and psychoanalysis can be: the imaginary is effective, it is material—but it includes ideals (ideas, images, projections) and it is different from the real, the inaccessible ground of the material. In his book *Postmodernism*, Fredric Jameson points out that Althusser's version of this fusion minimizes the question of the symbolic, another of Lacan's registers, and that the problem of critically charting our own imaginary relationships to real conditions requires the intervening mediation of linguistic representation. Ideology is not only imaginary representation, since it includes the communicating of those representations in words, images, and beyond, but at the same time, we must represent ideology in the symbolic (describe it, reveal it) to have any chance of changing its effects. Jameson's reminder of the symbolic is thus something like a call for new symbolic representations, for the work of mediating ideology.

We have seen that the concept of ideology encompasses several things: the distortion inevitable in every representation (in analogy to the optic nerve and the camera), the ruling ideas in a social context, false consciousness, and actions that produce social cohesion. We need to add one final dimension before moving on to our next key word, and that is the psychic compulsion which underwrites the actions that produce social cohesion. Slavoj Žižek embellishes Marx's explanation of the inevitability of ideology and Althusser's elucidation of ideology as practice with a specifically psychoanalytic sense of an ineffable, compulsive, spontaneous drive to actively accede to the given reality. In his view, which he derives from a combination of German philosophy with psychoanalysis, reality is a matrix of ideas and practices that provide coherence for the fundamentally incoherent raw material world, including the fundamentally contingent organization of that world into the capitalist mode of production. As he writes, "The function of ideology is not to offer us a point of escape from our reality but to offer us the social reality itself as an escape." For this notion of escape into reality, Žižek draws upon the contrast made in Lacan's psychoanalytic theory between reality and the real. Reality is a matrix generated by language, signification, images, and practices (the symbolic in Lacan's theory). The real is by contrast the limit to this matrix, an impossible, unknowable ground of reality that also undermines reality. Reality offers stability, the real destabilizes. Symbolic consistency, and the authority of any particular social order, work through acts of suture and imposition; encountering the real exposes these impostures. The real is sometimes thought of as a material substrate of what we know and do in social experience: matter, including the chaotic evolving matter of the universe, and drive, the force behind human activity and enjoyment. Reality is integrated; the real is unintegratable. Incoherence is hard to tolerate, and the vast terrain of undefined possibilities is terrifying, and thus there is something like a psychic and cognitive inclination toward manufactured coherence and delimited possibilities. It is this inclination which Žižek designates with the word "ideology."

Most emphatically, Žižek insists that ideology works by means of disavowal, renouncing or repressing a truth: we know that we live in an exploitative, contingent system, yet we act as if we do not know. This idea of disavowal is crucial for explaining how very direct admissions and very explicit displays of social truths of domination—like the widely circulated photographs of US torture of inmates at Abu Ghraib, or like Melania Trump wearing the infamous "I don't really care" jacket to visit the baby jail on the Texas border—make no change in the workings of power. Capitalist exploitation is not hidden; ideology is not the veil but the compulsive inertia of our keeping calm and carrying on. Thus, the real problem ideology poses is not how to precipitate enlightenment or raise consciousness, but what orthogonal or new practices conflict with business as usual.

Critique as practice

The theory of ideology has often straddled a line between a theory and a practice. Since Marx's *The German Ideology*, defining ideology has been entwined with revealing its social function, often in the manner of exposure: the young Hegelians thought they were radicalizing philosophy with their account of universality, but they did not consider that the Christianism of their notions supported the ruling government in Germany. Thus, the position from which ideology could be defined as the ruling ideas of the ruling class constituted itself as a critique of the ruling class. Critique had been Kant's name for a philosophy that tried to account for its own conditions of thought, and "ideology critique" became the accounting for the material conditions of many types of thought. Accounting for such conditions is the condition of possibility of transforming them. Marxism traces the rootedness of thought in social relations, and it also exercises the uprooting potential of thought, the power of ideas, deeply situated in context, to nonetheless take distance from their context, thus working to precipitate transformations. Critique is in this sense not an outside of context, but a possibility immanent in any context. Any given mode of production includes and confronts the real possibility of other modes; a critical account of the specificities of the capitalist mode of production can also operate as a projection of something else. Marxist theory is above all else this procedure of immanent critique, critique internal to a situation which speculatively effectuates new situations.

Under the leadership of the Frankfurt School, the critique of ideology took shape as a concerted project to oppose all domination by exposing the work of ideas and representation in its legitimation, and could thus be applied not only to the analysis of dominant culture but also to the analysis of academic, philosophical, and political discourses that purported to oppose some types of domination while explicitly or implicitly supporting other types. Often, ideology critique has addressed itself to a project of "demystification"—of revealing the mystifications, obfuscations, distortions in dominant ways of thinking. The wealthy are virtuous, the capitalist mode of production is natural, social inequality is inevitable—these are claims ripe for demystification. But in other versions, ideology critique has regarded most representations of social existence as necessarily balancing mystifications and illuminations, justifications and questions, ideology and critique. Ideology critique of textual or linguistic forms—speeches, literature, scholarship, verbal arts—requires some different tools than ideology critique of visual and practical forms—habits, institutions, architecture, painting, billboards. Whatever the medium of the cultural product under consideration, ideology critique is less the diagnosis of that product's particular ideology than it is the engagement with the product in order to reckon with the ideology of the social field outside the product. Thus, the goal of ideology critique is never simply to show how an artwork is secretly ideological but rather to confront the ideological web which the artwork and the critic alike are constituted by and are endeavoring to understand. Ideology critique interrupts the smooth normality of ideology, rearranges accepted meanings, and forms new categories, and the very process of so doing—collectively, say, in a classroom—may be an example of the kinds of practices that counter everyday practices of holding the mode of production in place.

Critique, the critique of critical criticism and the ruthless critique of everything existing and the utopian projection of something better, emerges within Marxist theory as one such practice for conflicting with business as usual. It is an unfinishable practice, an orientation toward everydayness as well as to large-scale history, to the imperative of social transformation, to the creativity at the core of the human.

Within the theory of ideology, we have seen this practice hailed as substantively *intellectual*: as reading, writing, studying. Marx recommended the materialist writing of history as the only way to apprehend ideology. Similarly, Lukács recommended investigation. Althusser also has a recommendation: "symptomatic reading." The critic of ideology must engage in a reading procedure which relates the manifest text (of a film, say) to a latent context (what he called "a different text, present as a necessary absence in the first").[17] Symptomatic reading is active, generative reading; it produces interpretations by linking what a text says and represents to the gaps in what it says and represents, and thereby generates an account of contradictions, negations, or other limitations that may have precipitated the gaps. Contrary to how it is sometimes caricatured, symptomatic reading is not "gotcha" reading that exposes a hidden meaning. It is rather a reading that situates, that places the text in relation to logics that overdetermine what can be said and thought, and that thereby helps those logics become traceable or nameable. It has a complicated topology: the logics are not extraneous outsides of the text but dimly perceptible insides. As Althusser memorably puts it, "The invisible is defined by the visible as *its* invisible, *its* forbidden vision: the invisible is not therefore simply what is outside the visible . . . the outer darkness of exclusion—but the inner darkness of exclusion . . . all its limits are *internal*, it carries its outside inside it."[18] Reading symptomatically is reading for shading and shadows, the framing and lighting of representation. When it comes to film, reading lighting and cinematography may therefore be an analogous procedure.

Symptomatic reading is especially well suited to reading *narrative* artworks. This priority of narrative has been elaborated by Fredric Jameson, a theorist who enhances Althusser's theory with more structural focus on narrative: in representing social relations, ideologies lend causes and closure to those relations, in the fashion of narrative grammar (a narrative requires a cause; a fact like "the sky is blue" is not a narrative but a statement of a cause of the fact or of the fact as cause is ("the sky is blue because of air pollution")). Ideologies give us causes for why things are the way they are, and they propose resolutions to the conflicts they acknowledge in that state of things. Studying narratives, such as novels and Hollywood cinema, therefore opens up new insights into how ideologies work, and reciprocally, studying narratives requires engaging with the problematic of ideology.

Across the different notions of ideology we have rehearsed here, a sameness stands out. Whether ideology is inversion, falsity, legitimation, interpellation, or disavowal, it functions to constitute a matrix for action: for what we do, for why we do it, for what we produce and reproduce when we act. It is in this respect an ultimate projection: ideology projects a reality in which our actions are purposeful. We will soon explore the formal analogy to cinematic projection but let us quickly posit at the outset that there is a dialectical counterpoint to this projection of reality within which we uphold capitalism: utopia. Thinkers ranging from Ernst Bloch to Paul Ricoeur to Slavoj Žižek have argued for a connection between ideology and utopia. Projecting a reality is after all not so different formally from projecting another reality, a better reality. Ideology critique seizes upon this utopian dimension. And, as we will elaborate later, the cinema as projective technology does too.

Ideology has been at the heart of the academic study of both high and low culture. If there are prevailing frameworks for social reality that hold in place an iniquitous mode of production, those frameworks might be identified in their concrete sites of production and circulation. Mass culture—music, TV, film, advertising—would seem to be a central such site. At the same time, if the ruling ideas belong to the ruling classes, then elite culture could also be central. Thus critics, historians, sociologists, and philosophers interested in the problem of ideology have often set out to interpret individual works of mass cultural production as well as individual works of high art. Yet because culture is traditionally understood as cultivation, beauty, civilization, a dialectical approach to the ideology of culture considers any given work's ambivalent function in propagating the status quo and in gesturing toward utopian alternatives.

The ultimate point of the Marxist theory of ideology is that ideas, which seem to be abstract spiritual entities in a different realm than concrete material activities, are actually material processes. They are not merely determined by those processes nor are they merely reflections of them. Ideas themselves are generative. What they generate may too often be the reproduction of the order of things, but they may also generate materializations in social practice that in turn generate the production of new socialities. The task for the Marxist critique of ideology, or the Marxist critic of film, is to explore what a given idea or representation makes possible, and what it renders impossible. It is also to practice these critical reflections as part of a social movement for transformation. A goal, then, of Marxist criticism is not only to appreciate or evaluate cultural production but to enter into conversation with cultural products in order to produce situated knowledge, which is itself a factor in the war of positions.

Just as the Marxist theory of ideology originates in reflections on the camera, the signal moments in the development of that theory often implicitly or explicitly refer to imagistic production. Ideology can be thought of as photographic or cinematic: the projection of an inverted image of the pro-filmic world, the phantasmatic wholeness of perspective, the inner darkness of exclusion, the screening of alternatives. These formal and technological similarities make the medium of cinema a rewarding focus for ideology critique. Indeed, today's foremost Marxist theorist of ideology, Slavoj Žižek, very often analyzes films for just this reason.[19] Through formal analysis of this type, film theorists can ensure that such critique is never merely the rating of a film ("*Mama Mia* is so ideological") but the situated grappling with how representation simultaneously conceals and reveals social contradictions.

Mediation

If ideas wield material force, a dialectical approach regards that force as working in two directions simultaneously: ideas uphold the ruling classes, and ideas critique the ruling classes.

"Mediation" is the Marxist name for this bidirectional capacity of ideas, representations, and forms. This Marxist inflection builds on diverse connotations of the term, from ancient philosophy, where it means communicability and finding a middle, all the way to contemporary media theory (which is particularly important for film studies). As long as this history of the concept is, it has remained relatively underutilized in Marxist analysis and especially in aesthetic and film analysis, so my discussion here will be less anchored in the history of the idea than our other two sections, and more driven by directions that film and cultural theorists should take up.

In everyday parlance, we know that "to mediate" means to create a relation—to, most commonly, facilitate a connection between two opposing parties. If we want to turn this verb into a noun, we could think of a "mediation" as a relating, a relation. A relation can be between two things by way of a third, but it can also be between the two things by way of each other, or between a thing and itself. In Marx's theory, which we have already noted is centrally concerned with form, we can understand "mediation" as the work of forms. The commodity form, the money form, the novel form, the state form, etc., are all mediations of the underlying class relations of the capitalist mode of production. They are all what he often calls "forms of appearance" of relations—they give specific, concrete contour to the diffuse network of relations. We cannot see or touch the capitalist mode of production, but we can see and touch the forms that instantiate it. We cannot directly perceive our social relations—they are not immanently present to us—but a novel or a film can *re*present those relations. In this sense social forms like money or films *relay* the mode of production— they communicate it, they make it available for our study, they mediate it. Mediation is profoundly important to the process of understanding the capitalist mode of production and the process of projecting alternatives, since it facilitates and actualizes the reading and investigating and writing that Marxists exercise as critical practice.

The contradiction of labor and capital is mediated—at once managed and displaced, illuminated and obscured—by ideology. The mode of production is mediated by its concrete manifestations. The resulting relation can also become a new thing. Mediation is thus more complicated than reflection or reproduction—it is a dynamic relation of working on and through something, yielding something different at the end. Metabolizing in this way, taking things in and processing them, can be denoted by the etymological origins of mediation. In Latin, the word *mediatio* means intervention, intercession, and halving. From this original meaning flow senses of going between two poles, taking up a middle, dividing. Mediation is a relationship of independence as well as of dependence, of opposition as well as of connection. For Hegel, mediation contrasts with immediacy. He is concerned with the distance between the knowing subject and the known object, and ultimately refers mediation to the self-reflexive knowing (the subject knowing itself as object) in which a true philosopher engages. Mediation is fundamentally conceptual for Hegel, the process of understanding the world. Marx then critiques the insufficiency of this self-reflexivity since it had remained too immediate in considering the philosopher's consciousness but not his social circumstances. Just as Marx defines his materialism as the situating of Hegel's conceptual process within social relations, his refinement of the concept of mediation involves inflecting it with material, not just conceptual/ideal, content. And he extends the idea of the movement between thought and circumstances into his theory of labor, which, as we have seen, he defines as a mutual transformation of the human and nature.[20] Marx may have elaborated on this notion of the transformation of nature in his letters and discussions with Engels that prompted Engels's compilation of the *Anti-*

Duhring, which theorizes an activity, or what Engels also called a "dialectic," by which nature materializes itself, moving from potentiality to actuality: "A transition is made from the realm of non-sensation to the realm of sensation." In this sense Engels propounded a theory of nature as transforming, mutating, actualizing—as mediating—that later media theorists and ecological philosophers—from Gilles Deleuze to Jane Bennett and Bruno Latour—would run with.

Because mediation is so central as a condition of possibility for, as a topic of, and as an outcome of, Marxist theory, we can remark the special consequences of Marxist theory for aesthetic analysis. When we study forms like painting or music or cinema, we are studying mediation. The individual art works can carry us to other times or to distant cultures, but their primary function is not to inform us about those contexts. Instead, the function of art is to reveal the processes of representation that structure its composed relations and that structure the social field. In so doing, art is able to continue to be of interest in radically different contexts than that of its emergence. Marx was very explicit about this. In writing about art, he asks "From where comes the eternal charm of Greek art?" Wondering whether evolving economic context invalidates meaning, he poses additional questions:

> Is the *Iliad* possible at all when the printing press and even printing machines exist? Is it not inevitable that with the emergence of the press the singing and the telling and the muse cease, that is, the conditions necessary for epic poetry disappear? The difficulty we are confronted with is not, however, that of understanding how Greek art and epic poetry are associated with certain forms of social development. The difficulty is that they still give us aesthetic pleasure.[21]

Following Marx's line of questioning, Marxist theorists like Raymond Williams and Pierre Macherey have emphasized that a work of art is not a thing but a social process; works of art are being produced and reproduced over and over again. Even when a sculpture or a film is "finished," it can circulate in new contexts, new times and places, and occasion new interpretations which reveal additional facets of the original work. The Marxist emphasis on social context for art thus does not fix the meaning of art as a reified reflection of its society, but rather opens the field of relations in which art is always contingently intervening. *Fight Club* necessarily looks like a different work upon release in October 1999 than after the November-December 1999 WTO protests in Seattle, September 11, 2001, the financial crisis of 2008, or the 2016 global fascist insurgency. The film's ability to continue to be interesting across those different social events speaks not only to its artistic and intellectual complexity but also to the situatedness of the social process of interpretation.

Art's ability to continue to offer aesthetic pleasure in different contexts stands in contradictory relation to its determination by its own context of production. Marxist theory of art highlights this contradiction. This does not mean that interpretations of individual art works must themselves be contradictory or equivocal. It means rather that interpretations must attend to how contradictions of cultural production and of the capitalist mode of production shape the individual work, including whether the work itself stages contradictions, and it means that interpretations must be conjunctural, recognizing their own situation.

Hegel, Marx, and Adorno all used the German *Vermittlung*, the putting of things into the middle, and "mediation" is frequently used (without definition) by critics discussing oppositions: the mediation of abstract and concrete, of subjectivity and objectivity, of past and present. Adorno accentuates the contradictory status of this middle: mediation for him is the awareness of difference/non-identity, of antagonisms/contradictions. Rather than the three-party mediation or two-party mediation, he thinks of the one party: "Mediation is in the object itself, not something between the object and that to which it is brought."[22] He contrasts mediation with the immediacy he sees in Walter Benjamin's correlating of superstructure causally to a substructure, and describes that immediacy as "romantic."[23] And he goes on to insist that "immediacy itself is essentially mediated."[24] Raymond Williams usefully posited mediation as "a positive process in social reality," stressing the varieties of agency in the "interaction between separate forces" that is the "relationship society and art."[25] Where many critics have interpreted the base-superstructure model and the idea of determination to mean that the superstructure is just a mirror image of the base, Williams insists on the interrelation between base and superstructure, and their mutual constitution by ongoing social practices, and therefore on the ways that there is no stable thing to be reflected in the mirror. Charting the different valences of "mediation" as intercession, reconciliation, indirect connection, he promotes it to describe the relationship between society and art. Rather than reflect society, art projects it, negates it, distorts it. Each of these operations of representation in turn engender other kinds of processes: social interpretation, pleasure, confusion. Just as Marxism conceives of the communist future as an outgrowth of the capitalist present, it allows that aesthetic representations do more than reflect the conditions and context of their production; art acts upon extant relations, even and especially when it projects inexistent relations. Nathan Hensley observes that mediation indicates "productive reconfigurations and critical recoding operations—that is, acts of thinking—texts themselves perform."[26] In media studies, mediation may be thought of as the filtering of reality into consciousness by way of differing technologies. In media theory, we find the Marxist insight that representation is itself part of the social process of the mode of production, since theorists argue that print, painting, photography, film, CDs, memes, etc., not only circulate but also transform experience. John Guillory argues that the very concept of media as communication was only able to be formulated with the invention of printing technologies, and that as the concept expanded, it enfolded the fine arts and information genres. For Marshall McLuhan, any new medium defines itself with regard to the medium it sees itself as superseding. Cinema understands itself in terms of the novel. The novel understands itself with regard to the newspaper. Mediation for him thus combines an object's differential self-identity with technological change. Richard Grusin accentuates Engels's natural overtones by arguing that mediation is "ontogenetic," pertaining to the development of being in nature, and therefore a notion which actually overcomes the dualisms previous thinkers relied upon in their definitions of mediation as a movement between language and reality or subject and object. For him, mediation "can no longer be confined to communication and related forms of media but needs to be extended to all human and nonhuman activity."[27]

A crucial Marxist formulation of the operations of mediation comes from Jameson's concept of "cognitive mapping"—a concept which has special ramifications for film theory. Art as social practice can take the shape of promoting social literacy, and the analogy of cartography works to indicate the orienting and projective function of such literacy. While the term "cognitive mapping" might court literal impressions that art can help us make in our minds a map of this existing world, Jameson means something rather more complex by it. As he admonishes: "Since everyone knows what a map is . . . cognitive mapping cannot (at least in our time) involve anything so easy as a map . . . dismiss all figures of maps and mapping from your mind and try to imagine something else." The something else that Jameson is after is therefore a less literal, more abstract process of social interpretation.

This process of interpretation takes place in the relationship between art and criticism. As Jameson makes clear when he first introduces the notion of cognitive mapping in his classic *Postmodernism, or, the Cultural Logic of Late Capitalism* (1991), art can teach (following the classical rhetorical tradition's definitions of art as able not only to delight or to move, but also to teach). Art can teach about "the true economic and social form that governs experience" and can teach about alternatives by its agency to "produce the concept of something we cannot imagine." But in order to do so, art needs criticism to pave the way since criticism illustrates the relations between social forms in positively existing reality and the imaginative forms that produce something else. Art that participates in cognitive mapping therefore needn't itself be literal or even didactic. It doesn't need to depict the geopolitical world of capitalist relations in order to mediate them. Rather, cognitive mapping results from aesthetic experience that promotes dialectics, abstract synthesis, or ideology critique.

Since cognitive mapping is a spatial metaphor for mediating the capitalist mode of production, it may be especially evident in spatial art forms. Thus, Jameson studies architecture at great length, but, significantly for our purposes in this book, he also takes up the idea that cinema is a fundamentally spatial art. In *The Geopolitical Aesthetic: Cinema and space in the world system* (1992), he foregrounds this spatial quality as central to film's ability to "think a system so vast that it cannot be encompassed by the natural and historically developed categories of perception with which human beings normally orient themselves" (2). Set design and projection are spatial relations that make up the cinematic medium, and that assist in cognitive mapping of the integrated space of the capitalist world system, the effort "to figure out where we are and what landscapes and forces confront us in a late 20th century whose abominations are heightened by their concealment and their bureaucratic impersonality" (3). Films that explicitly tackle the capitalist mode of production on a global level, like *All the President's Men* or *Three Days of the Condor*, often do so, Jameson argues, by intensifying their spatial aesthetic, creating unique shots and angles and plots attuned to setting, landscape, architecture, transportation, and telecommunication. Incorporating the medium's inherently spatial qualities into figurative studies of space, such films invite connections between local and global, concrete and abstract, in a dialectical fashion.

Marxist mediation ultimately names the dialectic that is proper to representation. Individual works of cultural production, like poems or films, mediate their socio-historical context, the dominant ideas of their time, and other works to which they allude or draw upon. Yet we can also speak of mediation as the action of culture as such, the processing of the mode of production into a meaningful reality and the taking up of distance from that reality. How does film mediate the contradictions of the capitalist mode of production? How does the projective technology of cinema reveal the projective function of ideology? What are the technological connections between the retina, the camera, ideology, projection, and the moving image? Mediation enables us to think of how films act upon the world ambivalently, making things apparent but also obscuring them.

Marxist film theory

If my general argument that Marxism is a theory that encourages constructive praxis is convincing, and if my outline of the core concepts of mode of production, ideology, and mediation has laid the ground for some important connections between Marxist theory and the theory of art, then we can now to turn to some more concrete ways in which it has enabled the analysis of artistic composition with regard to the ultimate composite art, film. Marxism can help bridge the gap that has recurred throughout twentieth-century film theory, between the study of film aesthetics and the study of film as social practice, because it provides such a comprehensive theory of how aesthetic representation issues from, instantiates, and alters social practice.

One of the concerns of this book is to address a conundrum: early film theory engages deeply with Marxism, but contemporary film studies seems to engage hardly at all. This is partly due to the rejection of theory in favor of proliferating localized analyses. As is the case in literary study, a traditional home of film theory in the university, the methods of the past several decades have inclined toward "post-Marxist" repudiations of Marxist theory and post-1989 denunciations of Marxist practice, and the dominant approaches have been less theoretical than methodological. In keeping with the institutional, economic, and cultural power of science, these humanistic methods have tended to become more social-scientific, more empirical, more factual. Trends in this vein include computational humanities, the new descriptivism, postcritique, and, most importantly, New Historicism.

The dominance of non-Marxist approaches

Film studies today is dominated by New Historicism. New Historicism can be confused with Marxism insofar as both center the analysis of art and culture on the social context. But its major theorist Michel Foucault, and its founding practitioners Catherine Gallagher and Stephen Greenblatt, were highly critical of Marx and Marxist theory, directly espousing the replacement of key Marxian concepts by alternatives that belong to a different way of understanding the world. Where a Marxist identifies "the capitalist mode of production" as the structuring tendency of modern social relations, a new historicist uses the more diffuse notion of "power." Where Marxists emphasize that social relations are organized under capitalism in contradictory ways, New Historicists underscore that "a system of power . . . (is not) as easily vulnerable to its own contradictions."[28] Where Marxists analyze causality and determination, new historicists analyze networks and distributed agency. Where Marxists prioritize the class struggle and a revolutionary transformation of the mode of production, new historicists track strategies of subversion and of containment. Where Marxists synthesize the particular and the general, New Historicists privilege the particular. Where Marx's own thought and the early Marxist film theorists promote the study of form, new historicists equate artistic form with other non-artistic discursive representations.

Among all these differences between Marxists and New Historicists, the most decisive is likely the contrast between dialectics and complexity. New Historicists affirm the complexity of power relations, the ambiguity of social practices, and the multifariousness of historical circumstances which demand granular accounting. Marxists regard the complex social field as simplified by the capitalist whole; interpreting from the point of view of this intensive whole means counterbalancing the particulars of historical circumstances with the generalities of historical tendencies. Dialectics is this interpretation with the aid of synthesis, a focus on contradiction rather than complexity, on the common cause of contradiction rather than its manifold manifestations.

In exploring what Marxism offers film theory, this difference between New Historicism and Marxism is crucial. A history of film theory might easily overlook this difference, since the distance between formalist approaches and contextualist approaches seems much more substantive than that between different kinds of contextualisms. Yet a big element of the argument in the remainder of this book is that contemporary film theory has been dominated by New Historicism without Marxism. This has impoverished film studies, ignoring the many resources in Marxism—especially dialectics—which can effectively integrate formalist and contextualist approaches. In the second half of the book, to which we turn shortly, I argue that a contemporary classic like *Fight Club* demands Marxist dialectical theory in order to make sense of how its formal achievements effectuate its political critique.

In film studies, New Historicism enmeshes film with other kinds of representation, like speeches by presidents, legal rhetoric, programs for film festivals, bestselling memoirs, and fashion editorials. Film is not a distinctive medium so much as a one among many vehicles for the promulgation of discourse. Analysis of films performed through this approach therefore concentrates on showing the continuities or discontinuities between a film and the broader cultural field, such as how a film set in a suburb populated mostly by Asian-Americans reiterates or undermines the housing policy in that region, how a film about the US special forces in the Middle East perpetuates narratives accompanying a 2011 rise in military spending, how an action film with a female director and female protagonist surprises marketers. These juxtapositions are important, and they are exercises of a version of the Marxist procedure of taking account of the context of ideas. But when they incline critics to point out parallels rather than produce interpretations of mediations, they become rote. The Marxist project of critique is still a good model of how to counter such roteness since it includes dialectical consideration of the utopian aspirations amid ideological distortions, of the position of the critic amid institutional relations, of the power of film form to complicate film content, of the mutually constituting and mutually exclusive relationship between consuming representation and participating in collective political action.

As opposed to dialectics, New Historicism pursues particularisms. The dominant New Historicism in film studies means that most scholarship on film is particularizing. When so much scholarly energy is expended upon connecting the particulars of one film to the particulars of a broader discourse, this is in keeping with the new historicist rejection of generalities. They revise the Marxist imperative for considering situatedness into a prohibition against what transcends the specific, local, embodied nexus. Generalities are presumed to be biased and hubristic (ethnocentric, phallocentric, exclusive), part and parcel of systemic domination, while particularizing is humble, ethical, and political. Marxism itself is understood as a bad generality, a "grand narrative" that pretends to a definitive account of history and social totality. Taking exception to the norm, disrupting the general, and cataloging the particular come to appear as political tactics common to cultural critics and direct activists. In this rubric, a new historicist reading of film limits itself to analysis of a particular film, to the exclusion of theorizing about and with film. Yet the particularism is also strangely unspecific since it combines interest in economic conditions of production with interest in empirical contexts of reception, diminishing the textual dynamics of film form. The practice of film criticism can then become random, rather than systematic, and, worse, it becomes cut off from other ways of making sense of the world. When we abstract from analysis of the particular to make some claims about the general, we construct a schema for connecting to other fields and other audiences. Even though New Historicism's juxtaposition of multiple discourses would seem to enable making connections of this kind, helping the film expert engage the anthropology department, a more theoretical basis for the connections— one dedicated explicitly to constructing concepts and generalizations—can do so more effectively.

The dialectical procedure that Marxism offers film theory also has consequences for the future of film production and film practice. Critique of the cinema expresses desires and proposals for what the cinema itself can become. It attends to the possibility that films can operate as immanent critique, a critique emergent from the form itself. It studies film form as the site of film agency. It suggests avenues for the production of a critical cinema. This future orientation is a logical complement to historical materialism's attention to the contingency of the past. Such futurism also opens doors to new collaborations between film theory, film production, and political practice. The meanings for this world don't simply exist; the workers who are artists and intellectuals, and the workers who are not recognized as such, can produce new interpretations, new representations of imaginary relations to real conditions of existence, and indeed new conditions of existence.

The capitalist phantasmagoria

Despite the dominance of non-Marxist and non-theory approaches in film studies today, there is a rich, early history of film theory's connections to Marxism that we can revisit as part of arguing for renewing Marxist film theory today. Marxism and film theory have close commonalities, owing to the kinds of conceptual problems they tackle. For Marx, a key to understanding the capitalist mode of production is fathoming the contradiction between the world of appearances and the world obscured by appearances. This is not a simple opposition between how things look and how they are, but rather a complex analysis of how the phenomenal experience of everyday life is at odds with the structuring principles of that life. We encounter a commodity, like a pair of sneakers or an iced latte, and the bounded contours of the object incline us to think that the object exists for its own sake, possessing intrinsic properties. The shoes are cool; the latte is delicious. It is hard to hold in our head the thought that the coolness is the product of the labor of marketers, designers, seamstresses, and rubber harvesters, that the latte is the product of early rising baristas, ice-maker mechanics, and foreign farmers. This difficulty means that our experience is akin to constant, instantaneous encounter with free-floating chimeras: we see, use, and enjoy commodities without the ability to integrate them into the relational system that produces them. Marx opened *Capital* with this befuddling phalanx of images: "The wealth of those societies in which the capitalist mode of production prevails, presents itself as 'an immense accumulation of commodities,' its unit being a single commodity. Our investigation must therefore begin with the analysis of a commodity." The image parade preoccupies theorists of many aspects of modern capitalist life, from Walter Benjamin, in his description of the architecture of shopping in Paris, to George Simmel, in his account of the sensory and corporeal stimuli of urban life. These and other theorists linked this parade of object-images to the "phantasmagoria," an eighteenth-century projection technology that prefigures the cinema. From the Greek "agora" (forum, assembly) and "phantasma" (ghost), the phantasmagoria used paper lanterns, lit from behind, to project images onto screens or walls. The lighting-lantern apparatus was often placed on a movable cart, allowing the creation of the effect of a moving image. The idea for these theorists, from Marx onward, is that the experience of life in modern capitalism is structurally comparable to the experience of the cinema. The spectator who beholds the moving projection experiences in distilled form the bewildering contradictions between appearance and essence in capitalism. As the famous Situationist activist and filmmaker Guy Debord adapted Marx's opening line in his account of the twentieth century: "In societies where modern conditions of production prevail, all of life presents itself as an immense accumulation of spectacles." We are spectators receiving projections without a full picture of how the projections are made. Cinema can therefore reveal to us this condition of our sociopolitical and intellectual experience. It mediates everyday phantasmagoria into moving pictures, giving a bounded form to the diffuse social phenomena. Moreover, cinema that exposes its own conditions of projection or production, through techniques like conspicuous stylized editing or lockdown shots, dutch tilts, and breaking the fourth wall, can teach audiences that the world of appearances is itself produced.

Given this affinity between the Marxist emphasis on contradictory appearances and film theory's emphasis on the production of appearance, it makes sense that one of the very first theorists of film to conceive himself as such was a thinker deeply invested in Marx: Sergei Eisenstein. Associated with the first ever school of film, founded in Russia in 1920, Eisenstein wrote one of the very first works of film theory in 1923, "The Montage of Attractions." The concept of "montage" named for Eisenstein the dialectical character of the cinema: it is an assembly of different parts, sutured together into a whole, with seams still apparent. The power of cinema to convey ideas derives from this interrelation of different shots, above and beyond the content of any individual shot, so that cinema formally resembles a dialectical idea/the dialectical method.

Eisenstein exemplifies his own theory better than any other filmmaker. The masterpiece of montage filmmaking is his own *Battleship Potemkin* (1925), a film that uses montage to connect the oppressive working conditions endured by sailors to their eventual revolt. The film additionally uses the technique to illustrate the bond between the revolting naval sailors and the people of Odessa who have no ostensible relation to them. In turn, Eisenstein hopes to trigger a similar enthusiasm for revolt among the spectators who see the montage at work.

Montage theory anticipates later structuralist theories of language and literature, which locate meaning in the relation among elements in a system, rather than intrinsically in the discrete elements themselves. However, Eisenstein also regarded individual parts/individual shots as themselves dialectical, since the pro-filmic event and mise-en-scène necessarily derived from the capitalist context of contradiction, and since the pairing of sight and sound could provoke sensory contrast and the sensation of contradiction. Shots are after all composed of lighting, depth of field, and sightline, a highly coordinated activation of formal elements. Thus, he distinguished the dialectical energy of montage from the mere complexity of continuity editing. Montage animates the succession of images, it activates their collision—it doesn't merely line them up. Eisenstein based his definitions of the film medium upon this implicit promise of dialectical art: montage is at its best something like an art of contradiction, formalizing the contradictions in the social world.

Eisenstein saw in film the prospect of representing collective agency, rather than the individualist acts of the theater. His principle of montage and his composition of frames were devoted to the actualization of a collective: more than one person in a shot, making masses into protagonists, de-emphasizing plot so as to prioritize collective characters in their interrelation and their connection to setting, connecting individuals to their environment (in some cases, his actors literally wore pieces of the set such as buildings or trees, attached to their bodies). He perceived, as well, that the medium of cinema was produced only from collective endeavor; that "from the first faint, glimmering hint of the theme down to a decision on whether the buttons on the leather jacket of the last extra player are suitable for filming purposes," film is the concerted effort of a collective.[29] We will return to this consideration of film's constitutively collective form in our discussion of the politics of the medium.

Eisenstein's work in establishing the theory of film crucially emphasized film form and gave priority to the capacity of the medium of cinema to show how reality itself is cinematic: a constructed, produced, formed series of images that often occlude their own construction. His theory is Marxist in combining an account of form with attention to political relations and the mode of film production. It is especially Marxist in expressing the power of the cultural object to critique the culture. These principles of mediation and of dialectical method should still ignite Marxist film theory today.

A contemporary of Eisenstein who also theorized film and identified as a Marxist was Walter Benjamin. In keeping with a Marxist emphasis on the determining function of the base, Benjamin considers how technological innovations like photography, the phonograph, the radio, and especially film transform the general idea of what art is. Specifically, the availability of photography radically revises the idea of art as a single object consumed under special circumstances and imparting an almost spiritual air of uniqueness. Because numerous prints can be made from a single photographic negative, the art of photography circulates multiply rather than singly, and can reach consumers where they are rather than requiring them to make a special trip to a single site to see a singular work. In Benjamin's view this results in the devaluing of the here and now of the work of art, decontextualizing the work, and diminishing what he calls an air of authenticity or "aura." The compromising of this authentic emanation desacralizes the work and the artist, inviting greater participation from the spectator. The positive side of this loss is therefore the democratization of art—more people can see it and can feel empowered to participate in determining its meaning. Film intensifies this democratic potential of the photograph since it enables not just moments but whole events or performances to be recorded and reproduced for wide audiences. The more art circulates, the more aura breaks down, the more the false attribution of meaning to genius, elites, and tradition is challenged, opening the way for the meaning of art to be understood as itself the product of social and economic processes of circulation, consumption, and interpretation.

The culture industry

Marxist aesthetic theory reached a great height in the years after the Second World War, when German Jewish intellectuals in exile in Los Angeles combined their experiences under the rise of Hitler with expertise in philosophy, sociology, and the arts, to articulate a theory of "mass culture." Mass culture connotes culture that is mass produced by industrial means for the masses, the majority of people, and effectively encompasses the shared values of most members of industrialized society. For example, the United States may be a nation of immigrants, and may even lack a common language, but its residents will share their exposure to popular music blasted at the grocery store, television shows involuntarily broadcast in taxis and at the gas pumps, billboards on the freeway and advertisements at the bus stop. This exposure amounts to a nexus of tacit, unthought values that circulate simply in everyday life. Theorists like Theodor Adorno and Max Horkheimer were especially attuned to the function of propaganda posters, rhetoric, and spectacle under the Nazis, and this primed them to observe a certain parallel in President Roosevelt's use of the radio and newspapers during the war, and to observe as well a parallel in the Los Angeles corporate studio system's industrial production of entertainment. As Adorno put it quite starkly, "Film has succeeded in transforming subjects so indistinguishably into social functions, that those wholly encompassed, no longer aware of any conflict, enjoy their own dehumanization as something human, as the joy of warmth."[30]

For Adorno and Horkheimer, the key factor of industrial art is that it is produced by industrial forces with economic interests in the system of business as we know it, and that the art emerging from this industry must thus promote the values that sustain the system. It is therefore less art than propaganda, propping up the ruling classes who control the industrial means of production. The ultimate value promoted by industrial propaganda is conformity, which fabricates a surprising unity amid the division of labor and secures the ongoing consent of the people to being administered instrumentally. Paramount among the propaganda technologies for controlling human beings is film, which cultivates passive spectators who conflate illusion and reality, and which tends to standardization in its aesthetic facets.

Adorno and Horkheimer argue that entertainment is part of the economic base of society. As they put it, "Amusement under late capitalism is the prolongation of work"; they argue that this work constitutes defending society. Similarly, they conceive this work of entertainment as a contribution to the forces of production: "The might of industrial society is lodged in men's minds." Mass culture shapes desires, and at the same time teaches us not to be fulfilled, and thus on both fronts it encourages a consumer mind-set that nicely corresponds to the industrial interests in selling ever more commodities. At the same time, artists who would be producers of culture are encouraged to think in terms of commercial success, and thus tend to conform to form and content trends already in place, to perpetuate what works.

The films of Frank Capra are exhibit A for the type of commercial cinema that Adorno and Horkheimer deride. Capra's films like *Mr. Deeds Goes To Town* (1936) and *Mr. Smith Goes To Washington* (1939) show the little guy succeeding against the big capitalist. But rather than call into question the capitalist system, this type of film ends up justifying the oppressive capitalist structure by showing that success is indeed possible for the oppressed class within it. In addition, Capra utilizes a hackneyed form that reliably leaves spectators secure in their position as subjects. For Adorno and Horkheimer, such security is precisely what art must disrupt.

Adorno and Horkheimer spend most of their time in negative critique, but they also see an emancipatory potential in art forms. They establish some criterion for art that is not merely reproducing the existing social values. Art must represent society in unexpected ways that allow for critical contemplation, and very likely will foment a sensation of dissonance—of contrast between the form and content, say, or of contradictory operations of forms, or of perspective that is detached from subject matter.

Adorno and Horkheimer's analysis historically anticipated mass culture in the United States since they were actually writing from the 1930s to the 1950s, before the industrial production and widespread dissemination of cable TV, corporate consolidation of news and entertainment companies, and home computers. Even though their concerns would thus be ramified by the cultural forms and practices which advanced in their late lifetimes and after their deaths, it nonetheless appeared to a subsequent generation of theorists that Adorno and Horkheimer had been too pessimistic about the political effects of mass culture.

Three significant turns away from Marxism in film theory

The impressively Marxist origins of the earliest film theories, as well as of theories that were internationally prominent in the decades surrounding the founding of university film studies, make it surprising that film studies today has so little to do with Marxism. Indeed, "Marxism" doesn't even appear in the indexes of two of the most prominent current theory anthologies for the classroom, Robert Stam and Toby Miller's *Film and Theory* and Gerald Mast, Marshall Cohen, and Leo Braudy's *Film Theory and Criticism* (each of which run 800 pages long). Perhaps all theories, especially those generated in the late twentieth century in the university, incline toward superseding themselves, and an inevitable renunciation of what comes before accounts for today's lack of Marxism. Perhaps Marxism has simply become part of film theory's DNA, no longer necessary to cite because it is so thoroughly in-built. Perhaps the general political repudiation of Marxism in the 1980s and 1990s fueled a search for other paradigms, for Foucauldianism and feminism and the postcolonial program. Perhaps the union of political and formal concerns in early Marxist film theory's attention to montage, editing, and protagonicity set the stage for film theory to present itself as an advance beyond formalism, which film studies seems to do with renewed vigor at every turn. Certainly, the field of film studies understands itself as "post-theory" (to take the title of one major textbook), dismantling universal questions of form, medium, and ideology and celebrating the particular.[31] This trajectory away from film theory and toward film analysis, focusing analysis on the auteur and the spectator, has frequently meant the sidelining of Marxist considerations with form, medium, production, and critique. Broadly we can identify three main currents of the turn away from Marxist (and especially Adornian questions), toward the putatively more "positive" subjects of cinematic and spectatorial agency: realism, auteurism, and cultural studies. Importantly, these non-Marxist trends coincide with the professionalization of film theory.

On account of the intense Marxist commitment to the social relations within which ideas are embedded, Marxist film theory not only involves the consideration of the conditions of film production but should also include some reflection on the institutional and economic conditions of film theory itself. The first bachelor's degree in film was offered at the University of Southern California in 1929. The UCLA School of Film opened in 1947. UNESCO, the United Nations organization dedicated to cultural production, commissioned studies of film as an educational, cultural, and political tool from 1954. The first scholarly professional organization, the Society for Cinematologists was founded in 1959 and it ultimately sponsored *Cinema Journal* (which began in 1968). The 1965 National Foundation for the Arts and Humanities Act evolved to found a federally funded American Film Institute in 1968. NYU awarded the first doctoral degree in cinema studies in 1973, in a program that included criticism, theory, and aesthetics among its subjects. Auteur theory legitimized the new discipline, since D. W. Griffiths or Alfred Hitchcock could be pointed to as parallels for famous composers studied in musicology, or famous painters studied in art history. Similarly, formalist theories of film underscoring the medium's intrinsic properties borrowed the model of literary formalism that the New Critics had employed to professionalize the independent discipline of English Literature. The earliest independent film departments claimed membership in the humanities even though the earliest film theories had social-scientific frameworks traceable to sociologies of mass culture and even to the House Un-American Activities Committee inquiries into the political effects of film. The institutionalization of film studies, the context for much production of film theory, is inseparable from the Cold War, UN soft power, and the new social movements. The kinds of interpretations film theory enables should probably themselves be subject to Marxist interpretation; film theories are parts of the superstructure, parts of the processes of social reproduction, and thus may reinforce some aspects of the capitalist mode of production while critically exposing others.

Perhaps it is no wonder, then, that Marxism ceased to be central to film studies since it is the theoretical and practical tradition which insistently calls out these contexts. The most prominent film theorists of the 1930s, 1940s, and 1950s broke significantly with Eisenstein and Marx, stepping away from film's formal capacity and its critical and estranging function, championing instead the objectivity and realism of the cinema. Thinkers like Siegfried Kracauer, a decided Marxist, and Andre Bazin, decidedly not, both underscored realism as the highest promise of film. In this respect they reactivated the original

intent of the earliest filmmakers, among them the Lumiere
Brothers in France and Thomas Edison in the United States,
to use film for informational and scientific purposes. For
Kracauer, the cinema continued a project in art history from
the Greeks onward "to record and reveal physical reality" and
this realism is fundamental to film, which "correctly reproduces
that part of the real world to which it refers."[32] Emphasizing
film's continuity with photography, Kracauer downplayed
montage, preferring instead techniques like tracking shots (in
which a camera is on wheels and moves through a contiguous
space) and establishing shots (long shots that show the spatial
context for a scene). Bazin shared Kracauer's appraisal of
the art historical trajectory toward realism, and Kracauer's
enthusiasm for the long take, and he added a priority for on-
location shooting. But his notion of realism alters Kracauer's
in that he allowed more technological intervention of the
camera, praising the realism that obtains in the camera's ability
to transcend an individual perspective. He extolled techniques
like deep focus, in which foreground, middle ground, and
background are all simultaneously equally sharply in focus,
and long shots, in which the camera is quite distanced from
its subject. As with both of these techniques, Bazin prioritized
depth of field rather than editing, since he believed the spectator
would then enjoy freedom of concentration; he opposed
techniques like superimpositions and dissolves since he saw
them as manipulations and artifice. For both Kracauer, with
his interest in the social reality of class struggle, and Bazin,
with his commitment to the ideal cinema, realism comprised
the basis on which to evaluate film's promise, political, and
artistic. But because realism has so often been understood
as the absence of form, this championing of realism diverted
attention from the film form dialectic.

   The history of film theory could largely be told through
the rubric of attitudes toward realism. This emphasis on
realism echoes a long tradition in Marxist cultural criticism
starting with Friedrich Engels and Georg Lukács. Engels
famously defined realism as not only "truth of detail,"

but also "the truthful reproduction of typical characters under typical circumstances," and Lukács consistently promoted realism's emphasis on typicality and totality as a more Marxist alternative than modernism's fragmentary ethos.[33] Socialist realism, an art and critical movement in the Soviet Union spanning most of the twentieth century, prized film that employed realist techniques in the service of representing the struggles and triumphs of the proletariat. For Walter Benjamin, cinema enabled a deepening perception of reality, and therefore tended toward democratic and critical possibilities. Writing in exile during the Second World War, Erich Auerbach celebrated realism as "the serious imitation of everyday life" and traced its democratic ethos across human history. Postwar Italian theorists and filmmakers like Antonio Gramsci and Cesare Zavattini advocated for a realist cinema that elevated everyday people and banal settings, propounding democratic sentiment.[34] After the Watts riots in 1965, students and faculty advocated for UCLA to establish an ethnographic track in its film school, promoting realist representation as a vehicle for social transformation.

Realism was also centered in the movement called "Third Cinema." A product of the 1960s revolutionary and anti-colonial movements in Latin and South America, these theories were most often developed by filmmakers themselves, who sought to overcome the merely entertainment function of films, instead promoting cinema as a technique of political struggle. The coiners of the term Third Cinema, Octavio Getino and Fernando Solanas, argued that Hollywood protocols, especially of big financing for commercial film and the 35 mm camera shooting 24 frames per second, could be contested by revolutionary cinema which they identified with realism. As opposed to beauty in its abstract tendencies, realism could, they argued, constitute an important part of decolonization, especially as it paralleled information technologies like journalism. Moreover, films that were guaranteed to be unsuccessful with bourgeois audiences—didactic films, testimonials, non-commercial forms—would amount to a fighting of the system. Technological changes in the medium, such as film that could be shot in normal light, could democratize production.

Filmmakers and intellectuals in other Latin and South American countries participated in this movement and expanded the theory. Fernando Birri argued explicitly that the underdevelopment of Argentina, the fault of colonialism, could be remedied by low cost cinema production intended for consumption by working class people, and privileging a realist or documentary aesthetic which could promote an accurate image of the people and their values. Even though other arts, like the Latin American tradition of protest poetry, could presumably be produced and circulated more easily and achieve the same political ends of precipitating critical consciousness, Birri's theory implicitly accentuated the intrinsic realism of the pro-filmic event, the medium-specific immersiveness of the spectacular art which doesn't require literacy. In Brazil, Glauber Rocha apparently worried that docu-realism would merely reinforce the colonizer's gaze regarding South Americans as primitive, and thus he advocated for representations of violence. In this view film that breaks with commercialism disrupts the usual values, and film that depicts revolutionary violence can revise the colonizer's gaze.

For many film theorists, realism will always be associated with film and film's potential. Even expressly fictional films may be theorized in terms of what they make legible in the real world. The philosopher Stanley Cavell rooted this essential realism in the technology of the photograph and the indispensability of the pro-filmic. For him film always carries the presence of the non-filmic world in ways which encourage the spectator's reconciliation with the world. In the post-2008 moment, critics like Leigh Claire La Berge and Alison Shonkwiler have identified a resurgence of realism in an effort to make sense of the global financial crisis. In Hollywood, this resurgence has even taken the form of several simulated documentaries about the crisis (*Too Big To Fail*, *Margin Call*,

The Big Short), and a real documentary about it won a 2010 Oscar. Realism continues to be widely regarded as a tool for understanding and even as a tactic for struggle, in ways that may explain the antipathy to film formalism and thus to Marxism in film theory. Indeed, the reigning new historicist methods of connecting film to other discourses in the cultural context and overemphasizing film story at the expense of film form tends to approach film as a reference to the world that is fundamentally comparable to other kinds of realist reference. For these theorists, film does not engage in mediation so much as iteration.

Parallel to this expansive emphasis on realism, the other move away from the Marxist origins of film theory is the reception-oriented emphasis on film consumers and their independent meaning-making, an emphasis that paves the way for the particularizing impetus of New Historicism. Beginning in the 1960s, critics associated with what is called the Birmingham School of Cultural Studies argued that Adorno and Horkheimer's work was too generalizing, projecting a monolithic mass culture without giving enough attention to concrete details of production and consumption. Figures like Raymond Williams and Stuart Hall advocated more research on audience reception, more historical detail on how specific companies, industries, and institutions go about their business, and more theories of cultural diversity and cultural ambiguity. The result of this more concrete research was a more fluid model of culture: some forms of art and media reinforce the dominant values of the dominant class, contributing to the domination of the working class, and some forms undermine that hegemony, providing ideas, narratives, and representations that can enable class struggle. Some forms do both of these things simultaneously.

The Birmingham School's prioritization of the range of possible political effects of mass media, and their insistence on combining methods and perspectives from multiple disciplines (history, anthropology, aesthetics) in order to produce a theoretically informed concrete analysis of culture, led the school to prioritize the political struggles taking place in the immediate contexts of media production and consumption. To understand a Hollywood film, for example, might mean attending to a screenwriter's strike in the year before its production, to a presidential election in the year of its distribution, to a local campaign for school curriculum reform in an area where spectator interviews were conducted. In this way they actualized an important aspect of Marx's own theory, the combination of critical analysis with a situated struggle for social transformation. But where the Birmingham school corrected the Frankfurt school's overly negative, overly general view of mass cultural practices, in some ways they over-corrected, prioritizing the "resistance" of individual consumers who made their own meanings out of texts above any coalescence or organization at a collective level.

This enthusiasm for resistant and oppositional consumption becomes especially tricky when the forms being consumed themselves directly thematize resistance. If Hollywood produces, through the capitalist means of production, a film which articulates a critique of capitalism, what kind of analysis is called for? How can the savvy consumer or the insightful academic evaluate whether the film is simply hailing a niche market to sell resistance, thereby reabsorbing those who identify as oppositional back into the position of passive consumer supporting the dominant relations, or whether the film provides genuinely inspiring and informative representation that can foment alternative social practices and fuel struggles? How much time must elapse between the consumption of the film and the exercise of this evaluation? Can any one critic be an expert in history and sociology and ethnography and formal analysis?

The massive scale of these questions about mass culture conduces to answers that prioritize context and circumscription. We cannot generalize a theory of film, we can only practice particular analysis: What does a particular scene or technique in a particular film do for a particular audience? No wonder the particularism of New Historicism became dominant.

Yet one-sidedness of any kind has continually proven to be inadequate in Marxist cultural interpretation, and indeed Marx's own methods elevated the dialectic. Rather than try to decide what side of the class war a particular film is on, we can instead emphasize the process of situated interpretation as itself a social practice, connected to other practices like consumption and struggle, but most importantly, ongoing in time. Interpretation does not get finished, because the context of interpretation keeps evolving. Moreover, we can underscore that the study of form need not come at the expense of context. Questions of what the medium makes possible, what it makes thinkable, what it mediates, can be formulated differently in different contexts.

The biggest non-Marxism is the biggest theory: Auteurism then and now

Along with these turns away from Marxism as too negative or too general, there is a constitutively non-Marxist strand of film theory that has predominated in both academic and popular circles for decades, and which is directly related to the spread of film as a serious art and the spread of film studies and film criticism as professional endeavors. As approaches were multiplying and other disciplines were taking film seriously, a theoretical position called "auteurism" emerged. Auteurism is the idea that film can be understood as the work of an author, a creative subject expressing himself. Instrumental in the institutionalization of film theory in the university, and the circulation of film theory through popular film clubs, film magazines, film journals like *Cahiers du Cinema*, and film festivals, auteur theory promoted taking the art of film seriously, exalting the director as an artist on par with painters and composers, and the work of film art as a manifestation of human freedom. Auteur theory can inspire formalist analysis since it may concern features of a director's composition that recur across multiple works and add up to a style. It has also contributed to popular esteem for and non-academic practices of film theory since it is the main perspective adopted by mainstream media publications and film buffs. Film reviews, film journalism, fan culture, and the award system all center on directors as the source of film's production. Academic books in film studies very often, to this day, organize their inquiries around individual directors. Auteur theory is generally widely operative today and serves as a baseline for New Historicism.

From a Marxist point of view, auteur theory is deeply problematic since it concentrates on individuals at the expense of collectives and contexts, and since it locates the cause of film form in genius rather than in social ideas. In many ways, the rise of the auteur is the decisive event in the story we are telling of the turn away from the substantively Marxist origins of film theory. After auteur theory, film is taken seriously, yet the root of its social power is relocated from the medium itself to the director. This paves the way for proliferating cultural studies which seat film power in the mind of the viewer.

After the worldwide anti-colonial and anti-imperial movements of the 1960s, some centers of film theory re-evaluated their auteurist turn. Even *Cahiers du Cinema* began to inflect its platform with more political and less existential content, applying the lessons learned from its celebration of film composition to formalist political analysis. It began to articulate film form with ideology and film criticism with the critique of ideology. The editors once took up Althusser's notion of symptomatic reading to argue for cinema spectatorship as "a process of active reading" which attended to "the internal shadows of exclusion."[35] There would seem to be an affinity between the attending to shadows and shading and framing that symptomatic reading practices and film formalism, scrutinizing the lighting and framing and composing of cinematic representation. And yet this blend of formalism and political critique did not take off. Instead, a differently Althusserian project gained ground, combining the consumer emphasis of cultural studies with the technological emphasis of media studies.

The apparatus

With a nod to Althusser's theories of the ideological state apparatus, this strand of film theory in the 1970s, arguably the transitional moment before theory ceded to film studies, focused on what it called the cinematic apparatus: the regulated interaction of the technology, the text, and the spectator. Just as Althusser suggested that ideology is a set of practices which mutually constitute the subject and the mode of production, apparatus theorists suggested that Marxist film theorists must consider the concrete practices in the cinema (projection technology, ticket sales, seating, concessions) and the way those constitute the spectator as a subject. Elements of formal interest like camera angle and lighting and set become important for apparatus theory insofar as they combine together to construct a point of view which interpellates the spectator. The spectator thus identifies with the technology to such an extent that she imagines that the film is her reality. Film is defined by apparatus theory as fundamentally homologous to the representation of imaginary relations to real conditions of existence—it is a machine for generating those representations, which works by identifying the spectator with the filmic perspective. This is especially true of generic Hollywood films, which prioritize omniscience and continuity editing; the point of view such films encourage spectators to adopt often amounts, Christian Metz argued, to a narcissism of prosthetic omnipotence.[36] Ella Shohat and Robert Stam have expanded this insight of apparatus theory to encompass how the imperial trappings of cinema perpetuate a sense of imperial subjectivity, a superior surveyor of the world as the camera flies.[37]

Apparatus theory involves studies of the difference between the formal point of view and structural interpellation in film versus video, in the theater versus the home, in *verite* versus computer-generated imagery (CGI). It also involves both the technology and the spectator, both the conditions of production and the conditions of consumption, and so it seems to work in more Marxist ways than does ordinary formal analysis. However, its materialist analysis tends to be theoretical rather than empirical (apparatus theorists did not do ethnographies at the theater, for instance), and thus often traffics in ideal spectators (prompting the charge from feminist theorists like Laura Mulvey that those spectators were male and that the apparatus was patriarchal). And, more significantly, it centers on the imaginary, little attending to those economic factors we have already identified as important for Marxist analysis: creative labor, the studio system, production financing, marketing, distribution, and sales.

The blind spots in apparatus theory illuminate the difficulties of practicing a truly Marxist theory of film. How much does a film's contribution to social reproduction hinge upon its formal, aesthetic properties (like point of view and editing) and upon its economic circumstances (like breadth of distribution)? If the spectator is essential, how can diverse processes of spectatorship be accounted for? Should film theorists interview real individuals, or does it suffice to hypothesize about potential spectators? Does a film's form interpellate a spectator, or does a spectator bring their own sense of agency to the table? Doesn't a Marxist account of the social activity of consumption need to be balanced with an account of the labor of production?

Both auteurism and apparatus theory tend to homogenize film as cultural practice into film as the expression of a genius, and film as the workings of a machine. In this way, these dominant trends in film theory encapsulate how un-Marxist most of the field has been. Marxist film theory, by contrast, reveals the heterogeneities within the work (the contradictions within film form), and relates them to the heterogeneities in the capitalist mode of production (its contradictions, and their mediations).

An alternate trajectory: Jameson and the prospects of Marxist film theory

Even as Marxism has been left behind by film theory, one theorist has continued to pursue its theoretical promise with such eminence that there is even an entire book in this Bloomsbury Film Theory in Practice series devoted to him: Fredric Jameson. The greatest actually existing Marxist film theorist, Jameson is generally known less for his film theory than his work as a literary critic since he is the author of dozens of books spanning a career from the 1970s to the present, most of which concern literature. But several of his works are collections of essays on film, while others treat film as a significant counterpoint to or revealing touchstone for analysis of literature, philosophy, architecture, art, and television. And more important than this quantity, the quality of his engagement with film wonderfully exemplifies the interpretative practice we advocate for in this book. In our overview of the key concept of mediation, we have already discussed Jameson's influential notion of cognitive mapping, which substantiates mediation as a process of understanding the world to catalyze changing the world. So let's now focus on another of his crucial concepts for Marxist film theory: periodization.

Jameson is perhaps most famous in literary and cultural studies for his contributions to what is called "periodization," an effort to describe large-scale artistic movements as they transform over the course of history. There are many approaches to periodization, but a Marxist one fundamentally starts with transformations in material history and within (or among) the mode(s) of production. This means that a Marxist periodization of literature considers economic changes like the enclosure of common lands or the development of global shipping as illuminating backdrop for changes in literary style or the advent of new literary genres. Yet in some sense these changes are not changes at all, since they extend more of the same: the capitalist mode of production. Thus, Jameson has remarked that "for Marx, modernity is simply capitalism itself," an equation that would seem to acknowledge that as long as we have capitalism, we are in modernity, not postmodernity.[38] A Marxist film periodization attends to the mutations in the capitalist mode of production since 1895, including the impact of the First and Second World Wars on global economic production, the large-scale shift toward participation by middle-class women around the world in the official wage, the end of Bretton-Woods in 1973, the founding of NAFTA, the development of the internet and subsequent dot-com boom and bust, and the global financial crisis of 2008. These shifts are the broader context for what historians of film identify as significant pivots, mainly technological evolutions such as the rise of digital video, or the advancing popularity (and enabling tax breaks) of filming away from studios in locations like New Orleans, Chicago, and Albuquerque. For a Marxist, periodizing schema are opportunities to ask new interpretative questions about the form, content, and ideology of film, but they are not answers to those questions. Film has a different relationship to capitalism than certain other kinds of artistic production, like poetry, since its history is entirely coincident with capitalism. How to understand this difference is also a question: Is film, as some might argue, the paradigmatic artform of capitalism? Does this mean it is incapable of imagining a beyond of capitalism, since it is a representational form conditioned by capitalism? Or does it mean that film has some special ability to mediate the capitalist mode of production?

As Clint Burnham describes Jameson's achievement in his book in the Film Theory in Practice series, Jameson's method of film interpretation is "always dialectical in two important ways: first, it seeks out the contradictions internal to a film and its workings, and then, in a way that brings us back to the question of periodization, it locates the film in a historical context or situation." This means that Jameson synthesizes the context and the text, reading film form in relation to economic reality. Furthermore, and this is a crucial point, Jameson's technique of periodization differs from the new historicist approach to context because he always integrates contextual particulars back into the general history of the capitalist mode of production. Periodization is a contextualism that keeps the general in view, fathoming big swaths of economic continuity and discontinuity.

This dialectical character of his regard for film, and the dialectical character of his philosophy of history, makes Jameson the critic whose work most consistently actualizes the powerful promise of Marxist film theory. This is in no small part because his overall prescription for critical practice is that it must be dialectical: "A Marxist negative hermeneutic, a Marxist practice of ideological analysis proper, must in the practical work of reading and interpretation be exercised simultaneously with a Marxist positive hermeneutic, or a decipherment of the utopian impulses of these same ideological cultural texts."[39] His analysis tends to keep in mind economic history, but to still begin with the form of a film, especially with what seems paradoxical or contradictory within its formal system, and how that formal frisson might be said to represent the social contradictions of capitalism. For example, he might argue that minor characters in a film set up the film's investigation of class politics since the tension between the minor and the major, which reiterates that between big-name stars and their anonymous character-actor counterparts, direct our attention to the social rules of who has power in society.

For Jameson, the ultimate point of the dialectical balance in method between formal analysis and economic contextualization is to arrive at a dialectical conclusion: many films present an interpretation of society—a representation of imaginary relations to real contradictions—that can function dually, as a re-inscription of the way things are, and as an articulation of utopian impulses for things to be different. Thus, Jameson takes the broad arcs of the Marxist theory of ideology as we have traced them and enhances the connections between the production of representation and the production of something new. Art, like everything else, is always ideological, but unlike everyday discourse, art makes the dynamics of representation itself a subject of investigation: art encourages us to think about how representations work, and therefore to think about what representation does in the world. When art is especially forward about mediating its own representational apparatus, techniques, and medium history, then it gives us to think this power and functioning of representation in vivid detail.

Some motifs in Marxist film analysis

Now that we have reviewed the history of Marxist film theory, we can summarize some consistent topics of Marxist film analysis. These topics must be taken up dialectically— in relation to one another, and with regard to the relation between any individual film and the medium of film as such—or the project of theory will dissolve into the localities of mere analysis. Marxist film theory upholds the singular indispensability of mediation: aesthetic representation always enfolds the possibility of immanent critique, of texts breaking from context, of forms alienated from their determination, of ideology exposing itself. Analysis of any particular film must tie back to this essential appraisal of filmic potential.

Because of Marxism's emphasis on the basis of culture in the capitalist mode of production, any practice of Marxist film theory will likely attend to the basic economic relations undergirding the production of film. Movies are big business, and big business in particular for a global order atop which the United States presides as hegemon. In the twenty-first century the US federal government's Bureau of Economic Analysis began trying to formally calculate just how big, and they released the first annual findings in 2013, estimating that Hollywood-led creative industries account for 3.2 percent of all US goods and services, or approximately $504 billion of GNP.[40] By comparison, tourism is only 2.8 percent. Hollywood is the largest employer in the entertainment industry, with an estimated 310,000 workers. The state of California is the world's fifth largest economy, around $2.7 trillion GNP, behind only the United States, China, Japan, and Germany; in that economy, Hollywood is smaller than Silicon Valley technology, but still accounts for $300 billion of that total.

Thus, it is important to understand that the United States has long been the dominant center of the film industry, even as its profits have been majority international since the 1950s. It is equally important that this center of the industry is organized by large conglomerates, many of which have been operating since the early twentieth century. These conglomerates include Walt Disney, Sony, Time Warner, Viacom, NBC Universal, and 21st Century Fox. One of these, Disney, ranks in the top 10 percent of Fortune 500 companies. All of these companies combine film interests with other industries, such as television, cable, telecommunications, and appliances. They also all function through vertical integration, meaning they control multiple levels of the production process, from purchasing scripts and acquiring film rights to novels, memoirs, and other patentable stories to shooting on sets in physical real estate they own to marketing through other industries they own (TV, newspaper, and radio commercials, for example) to distributing films among theater and retail chains they own.

These significant economic functions of Hollywood suggest that there is quite a lot at stake when a film challenges dominant corporate values. It is in the best interest of the film industry, the US economy, and thus the global economy, for Hollywood to continue turning sizable profits. These interests may make it unlikely that films seriously represent anti-capitalist ideas or practices. They provide important context when evaluating the messages of individual films, or when assessing whether it matters that some films are products of major, traditional, and/or integrated companies and others the products of small, untraditional, and/or independent companies. The economic facts of film production do not dictate the stories that films tell or the forms that films take. But they are determining—they set some important limits. One task of a film analyst working from a Marxist point of view is to discern and acknowledge those limits.

These limits set by the capitalist mode of production stem not only from the overarching industrial situation of Hollywood but also from the economy as a whole. Marxist film analysis should also situate the film being analyzed within not only the macroeconomics of film production (3 percent GNP) but also the more immediate economic context of its individual production. It is therefore useful for a Marxist analysis to consider the facts of a particular film's economic situation, including its production financing, its profits, what state the film industry was in at the time of its production, and how the global economic system in general was performing. A film made in the late 1990s, like *Fight Club*, may be influenced by the ways in which the industry was rapidly expanding in that period. The 1990s were the longest period of economic expansion in American history, and Hollywood grew alongside everything else. New levels of industry integration were enabled by the approval of mergers of major studios with television broadcasters, creating Disney as owner of ABC, Viacom (Paramount) as owner of CBS, and Universal/General Electric as owner of NBC. Feature films became more linked to post-theater branding ventures like videogames and musicals. Megaplex cinemas became more common, partly to simulate the free choice experience of cable television. As home viewing of movies escalated, Hollywood turned toward spectacular action, special effects, CGI, and performance stunt films that readily showcased the benefits of the large screen. Studios made use of their international conglomerations to initiate worldwide releases, generating more marketing buzz and global engagement. This successful expansion of the industry suggests that executives may have felt it less risky to take on idiosyncratic projects. We might say that capitalism's boom years enabled the flourishing of more critiques of capitalism, precisely because those critiques would seem so irrelevant. But the boom also meant that more begot more and same begot same; *Fight Club* was greenlighted as an action film and was marketed that way against its director's wishes.

Alongside the macroeconomic context that comprises the mode of film production, another aspect prioritized in Marxist analysis of film is the division of labor. We have seen that this notion arises to describe the tendency of humans to specialize in their creative activities, and the pressure of the capitalist mode for efficiency and autonomation and standardization. In film production, the division is also what makes the medium very collaborative. Some workers will help set the stage, as it were, for shooting: writing a screenplay, hiring actors (Casting Director), negotiating contracts, doing makeup, designing or purchasing costumes, arranging lighting, building sets, sourcing props, coordinating transportation of people and equipment to filming sites. Some workers will learn lines to be characters, learn blocking to be extras. Some will be involved in shooting, conducting the camera, positioning it (Dolly Grip), loading film or changing memory cards (Loader), getting perspective on how things are looking. Still others might never set foot on the set but will work hard on putting the film together: editing, splicing, choosing among different takes, synching the sound, choosing soundtracks (even composing or performing soundtracks), designing trailers, arranging promotional campaigns.

Some of these workers belong to professional guilds and unions, and sometimes these unions are involved in negotiations over their conditions of labor or are even on strike. The Writers Guild of America has staged two huge strikes in the past few decades, lasting over four months in one case and almost six months in the other, and both concerning how writers are compensated relative to the rest of the industry, especially with regard to post-theater viewing on DVD, streaming services, etc. The first ever Screen Actors Guild strike, which won the right for actors to earn compensation in residuals, was led by a charismatic young Illinoisan named Ronald Reagan. Film laborers may also organize themselves unofficially. Frances McDormand used her 2018 Academy Award acceptance speech to underscore that one answer to the sexual assault, harassment, and discrimination scandals plaguing the film industry and the economy at large is an "inclusion rider," a contract provision stars, writers, producers, and others can adopt to ensure equitable representation of, and compensation for, women and/or people of color in a film's production. Analysts of films produced in the coming years may attend to the impact of this kind of labor action.

Film production often involves a large spectrum of laboring types, from caterers to lawyers, graphic designers to publicists, financiers to celebrities. This in-built diversity of economic positions may mean that medium has some capacity for rendering that diversity available for consideration. Moreover, the collective nature of film production provides one explanation for how a film might contain contradictory messages (whereas it can be harder to get this when reading a novel). In cases like *Fight Club*, where there is a novelist, a screenplay writer, and a director, we may reflect that there are inconsistencies or complexities within the film that pertain to this plurality of origins, or even to the different class positions of the creators (*Fight Club* was the screenwriter's first screenplay, adapted from an unknown novelist's ill-selling first novel, but its director's third Hollywood feature film).

The industrial context for *Fight Club*, as for any movie, is not a key to the film's meaning but an indicator of questions that can be profitably asked of the film. Differentiating between the explanatory power of context and the suggestive power of context has often been a debate in Marxist cultural analysis. The term "vulgar Marxism" refers to the reductiveness of the explanatory tactic. The dominant New Historicism often contents itself with merely identifying context. A more dialectical Marxism, by contrast, wants to take account of the overdetermination of a film's meanings, and of the ways that cultural production exceeds its immediate context. After all, the issues of consumerism, alienation, corporate malfeasance, and workers' struggles that *Fight Club* explores are not specific to the 1990s but recur across the centuries-long history of the capitalist mode of production. The framing of those issues and the imagination of political possibilities around them can be very specific to a historical moment but can also repeat earlier moments or resonate with future ones.

After production comes consumption; another consideration for Marxist film analysis is thus the functioning of film as a commodity, a thing that is bought and sold, consumed and exchanged. We might think that going to the movies is an escape, something to do for leisure, and therefore far away from the workday or the normal order of capitalist society. Entertainment seems unproductive since it doesn't result in something that can be sold. I might write a review of a movie after I see it and post that review on Fandango.com, which might in turn earn additional profit by selling more ads since it has more impressions, but in general it is hard to see what I contribute to the direct economy by consuming a movie. But a Marxist perspective directs our attention to what is productive about consumption—to who profits directly from our ticket purchase, and to who profits indirectly. It points to the ways that the appearance of leisure or an escape can renew our capacity to work more; to the ways that the experience of enjoying a movie that seems to criticize dominant capitalist values can restore our faith that we are freely choosing to participate in the capitalist mode of production. Marxist film theory ultimately frames questions about how the consumption of arts commodities contributes to the social reproduction of the current state of affairs.

When, as in the case of *Fight Club*, a Hollywood film offers a critical perspective on the capitalist mode of production, the question becomes: Who profits from offering this perspective? Do those who profit control the hearts and minds of those who pay? Does the circulation of ideas provide fodder for new sociopolitical acts, or does entertainment deflate any will to act? When we watch a movie that depicts political struggle for social transformation, do we want to go out and generate our own struggle, or do we want to watch more movies? Marxist film theory does not prescribe answers to these questions, but it underscores that they should be part of the picture of any film analysis. Because many of these questions cannot be answered through film analysis, but rather would require things like ethnography and statistics and long historical distance, the mere posing of them highlights the ways that film analysis is its own situated, limited cultural production.

All of the considerations we have just outlined as crucial for Marxist film analysis—the connections between film production and the capitalist mode of the production, the conditions in the macroeconomy when a film is produced, the conditions in the film industry when a film is produced, the labor conditions and division of labor, the conditions of consumption, the position of the critic—require research into the socioeconomic context for film. The literary theorist Jonathan Culler has remarked "Meaning is context bound, but context is boundless."[41] The Marxist dialectic has the advantage of counterbalancing boundless context with the bounded text, and thus formal analysis must complement contextual analysis. The ultimate topic for Marxist film analysis is formalist analysis since it is in the form itself that we find the materialization of social contradictions and their mediation.

Film form

The contextual questions we have outlined for Marxist film analysis must be taken up in relation to film form. We have seen that formalist inquiry is essential to Marx's own thought, and in this section I make the case that it is equally essential to fulfilling the dialectical potential of Marxist film theory. As I have argued, this potential emerged at the very beginning of film theory, in the works of Eisenstein and Benjamin, but the evolution of film theory since then has been away from Marxist considerations and away from formalist ones. Renewing those projects is a goal of this book.

The tasks we've outlined for Marxist film analysis so far revolve around the economic base of film (the conditions of its production) so we must now articulate the interest that Marxist film analysis necessarily takes in film form. An elementary way to understand the form of film is as projection. We have discussed projective technologies that preceded film, such as the phantasmagoria, and we could also mention the map or the panoramic painting or abstract mathematics. From the Latin word '*projectum*' for "to throw forth," a projection is the putting forward of a plan or scheme, an imagination or conception, the casting of a representation into reality. The camera obscura projects light into its enclosed dark room, the cinema projects movement (as its Greek *kinema* signifies) by projecting moving images onto a screen. We have also discussed many theories of ideology which share in common the function of projection, starting with Marx's definition of ideology via the camera obscura and culminating in Žižek's notion of the projection of reality as an escape from the chaos of the real. Film form to a Marxist, then, may first of all be the conjuncture of technological and ideological. And this means that reading film form can be integral to the critique of ideology.

Films are formed using techniques of cinematography and editing, the creation of shots and the interrelation of shots. They are also formed out of the space of the sets, the bodies of the actors, the words in the script, and the sounds they incorporate (including music). Whether spoken by a narrator or a character, the words in a script may contribute to the film presenting a narrative. Since narratives often entail plots (the patterning of events) techniques like editing can become essential to how narratives function, creating causal relations or connections and disconnections. Narratives, however, are not the only way form can be seen to operate. Indeed, form may entail intertextual allusions, or moments of formal self-reflexivity, incoherence, and contradictions between content and form. A film that tells the story of empathetic relations between a white lawyer and a black client, for instance, might consistently use lighting and shot structure to distance the spectator from the black character, contradicting its superficial message. This is the strategy employed in the unfortunate *A Time to Kill* (Joel Schumacher, 1996). Something as subtle as the way that *A Time to Kill* differently lights the actors Matthew McConaughey and Samuel L. Jackson supports racist preconceptions while the narrative enables disavowing any racism.

Even though it seems obvious, it is necessary for formalist analysis to point out that feature films in the Hollywood system are generally fictional; this fictionality is an important formal consideration. Fiction comes from the Latin noun *fictio*, meaning the action of shaping or feigning, as a variant of the verb *fingere*, meaning to make or mold. It connotes something imagined, as opposed to something existing. We have seen that Marx's definition of labor very importantly encompasses imagination as an indispensable aspect of the productive process, so we must be careful in taking fiction as contrasting with something more real. After all, revealing the real world to be the product of contingent historical processes, and indeed to be the form of expression of a particular mode of production, is a core goal of Marxism. In this sense, then, Marxism helps us recognize the fictionality, the shaped-ness, of reality itself. And we have also seen in our discussion of ideology that imaginary representations of imaginary relationships are constitutive elements of the social structure of capitalism, that representations can be part of the base of the mode of production. Fictions can thus be very real.

Paradoxically, the realness of film fictions compels them to avow their own fictionality. Films frequently contain riders in their credits that avow "This is a work of fiction. Any similarity to actual persons, living or dead, or actual events, is purely coincidental." These are included for legal purposes, to indemnify against slander suits, but they have the effect of underlining the aesthetic and philosophical problem of where fiction meets the actual. When we analyze film form in terms of fictionality, we consider how the world presented in the film alters, differs from, and negates the world in which it was produced or is consumed. We attend to devices of fictional creation, like plot resolution or special effects. We address the consistency of the diegetic universe and reflect on the parallel constraints of our own context. Acknowledging fictionality also entails assessing whether the consumer/critic suspend their disbelief, or feign belief, or attribute belief to others, which are all key registers of the functioning of ideology; foregrounding fictionality in film form paves the way to interpreting ideology.

Film fictionality effectuates a different configuration of the conjunction of fiction and real than in other modes such as the novel, since film generally makes use of the pro-filmic setting, event, and persons. Brad Pitt the actor stands at the heart of the fiction of Tyler Durden the character, and that origin in the existing world leaves an irreducible residue in the fictional one. The philosopher Friedrich Nietzsche first identified this dynamic as pivotal for live theater, which relies on the body of the actor to generate the effect of character. Film intensifies this contrast between the fictional and the real, using not only actors but also spaces (like locations where films are shot) to provoke the sense of gap between the pro-filmic and the filmic. We might thus conclude that the medium of film primes us to behold the fictional nature of reality, that this is one of its in-dwelling theories. When we watch films, it is hard to forget that actors and spaces are being crafted into characters and settings; our awareness of this craft can redound to our awareness of the crafted quality of all identities and social environs.

Just as a film is made out of many different types of labor, the resulting entity is made up of many different elements. When we pay attention to form in our analysis, we are paying attention to these elements—to performance, to costume, to lighting, to music, to cinematography, to editing. The more descriptive, evaluative, and thoughtful the language of analysis is about these elements, the more its analysis rings true. But more importantly, we attend not just to these elements in isolation but to the interrelation among these elements. Film form is not just any particular aspect of formal composition but the dynamic connection between those aspects, the ways they work together to produce meaning, coherence, and even dissonance. For example, a film with a serious subject matter, like corporate malfeasance, whistleblowing, and mental distress, can propound entirely different meanings through its zany music, stylized sets, and sunny camera filters, producing an effect of tonal mismatch that it in turn deepens the meaning of the banality of evil. This is the way that Steven Soderberg's *The Informant!* (2009) articulates its critique of contemporary capitalism.

The importance of the fusion of the elements into form has prompted film theorists David Bordwell and Kristin Thompson to speak of form as a "system." Analysis of a film must engage the system, not just the components. When we decide what a film is about, we must incorporate not just its explicit meanings or the events in its plot but its mode of representation and use of its medium to enrich and complicate the explicit level. Treating form as system requires regarding the connection between the elements, and then going on to specify how those connections work. Are they relations of repetition? Or of difference? Do they tend toward resonance, or toward dissonance? How does the end confirm or overcome the beginning? When there seems to be an explicit meaning of one scene or sequence, is this reinforced or undermined by others? These considerations may be classified as "formalist," but their disposition toward the synthetic whole marks them as dialectical: dialectics balances the part and the whole, the particular and the total.

Formalism, the attention to the form of a film as determining its meaning, is often contrasted with contextualism, the attention to the conditions of production or conditions of consumption as determining its meaning. We have been arguing that a Marxist film interpretation must do both of these things, to avoid being reductive, to work dialectically, and to fulfill Marx's commitment to both social context and form. Thinking of form as a system, as a whole interrelation, further accentuates the Marxist interest in form, since Marxism as a point of view is often distinguished by its interest in the whole, in the tendencies of capitalism that structure every experience in this mode of production. Concepts we have seen like determination and mediation are ways of characterizing the interrelations of the whole.

Systematic formal analysis is of utmost importance when conducting political interpretation of a film. Formalism has often been characterized by competing schools of critics as the least political method since it considers the intrinsic composition of a film more than extrinsic factors like financing or reception, and since it has been associated with aesthetic appreciation and with aesthetic evaluation. (Is the cinematography beautiful? Is the performance masterful? Is the score profound?) But attending to form as system enables sufficient and convincing evidence for political interpretation. If I say, as several prominent critics have, that *Fight Club* has fascist politics because it depicts a long sequence of a populist insurgency with intense libidinal investment in a charismatic leader, that might be the basis of my recommendation that friends should not see it, or that professors should not include it on a film studies syllabus. But if my method of analysis obliges me, the way the form-system notion does, to consider how the fascism sequence fits with other sequences—whether it is the concluding sequence, how the lighting and shot-structure in the sequence affects its tonality, promotes or discourages identification with the characters, foments support for or distance from the events—then I can come up with more convincing evidence for my interpretation, one way or the other.

It is rare that cultural products are unambiguous in their political messages. Working with the form-system model as a complement to contextual analysis, Marxist film theory directs us instead to think about ambiguities and contradictions, and to esteem films that enable such thinking. It is less likely that a film supports fascist politics than that it makes fascism a topic of exploration. We can make a decision about whether the exploration on balance arrives at a position only if we take into account the whole film. But position-taking is less common in works of art than political art critics might like it to be, and for this reason the Marxist dialectical approach to film form should ultimately ask whether and how a film makes contradictions evident.

Most importantly, formal analysis enables the film critic to be methodologically precise in their claims. Film studies incorporates aspects of history, anthropology, sociology, and philosophy but at its core our methods for producing new knowledge stem from the interpretation of film. The contradictions of the capitalist mode of production could keep an ethnographer busy for years, interviewing studio executives about why they greenlit an ostensibly anti-capitalist film, interviewing novelists about whether they agreed with the screenplay adaptations of their work, interviewing fans about whether they changed their everyday practices or political values after seeing a film. But the contradictions in a film's form are circumscribed by its aesthetic finitude. Social phenomena are complex and diffuse; artistic phenomena are complex and bounded, and this boundedness is essential to the film theorist's ability to make a conclusive argument.

Why Fight Club?

I will turn now to the interpretative exercise that will occupy the rest of the book. This Bloomsbury series, Film Theory in Practice, is built around the idea of exemplary engagement with classics or contemporary classics—with films that might not appear on every History of Film syllabus proceeding through the greatest cinematic achievements, but which have commanded lavish attention from spectators and scholars in the past few decades. In choosing *Fight Club* for a book on Marxism, we have selected a film that very explicitly engages in and with theory. This means that many Marxist ideas are articulated in the film or provide fodder for the film's plot, which portrays two alienated white-collar professionals' engagement in alternative social relations that mushroom into more ambitious political projects, and a climatic revelation that the two are actually one person. But it also means that many ideas in Marxist film theory are underpinning the film's formal composition. In this way, our analysis of the film will have to be careful. We cannot presume that we bring theory to explain a film, that the film is an object to which we apply our masterful tools. Rather, we have to foreground the relationship of interpretation, the agency of the film in doing its own theorizing, the purpose of critical analysis as something other than exhibiting mastery.

Marxism and the camera emerge in the same historical conjuncture. Film theory is similarly entwined with Marxism, insofar as most of the first actual theorizing about film was performed by thinkers and filmmakers with Marxist sympathies. The exposition and arguments in this book are intended to help reinvigorate this mutually constitutive relationship by fostering more dialectical film theoretical practice. And there is no better way to model that practice than in conversation with a film that theorizes itself.

CHAPTER TWO

Marxist Film Theory and *Fight Club*

The importance of the dialectic for Marxist cultural criticism, and for its philosophy more broadly, means that it isn't obvious where to begin a Marxist analysis of a film. There are drawbacks and benefits to beginning with economic facts of production, and the same to beginning with describing the form. It is therefore important to foreground these complexities at the outset. Any film would raise this problem of where to start Marxist analyzing. The particular film we have chosen for this book, *Fight Club*, not only raises the problem but tries to provide guidance on where to start.

Most films in theaters show a logo for a production company as the very first frame on their reel. They then either show some action, or they roll straight into a credit sequence. *Fight Club* follows this standard of showing the logo for Regency Enterprises, a film, television, and distribution conglomerate founded in 1991. But then it rolls three seconds of a dark screen with just a little color in the background, and some orchestral music, suggesting that a scene is about to take place—that it has chosen the option of establishing some action before interrupting with the credits. However, in the fourth second, the sound of a record scratch is heard, and the music abruptly switches to heavy electronic rock. At the same time, words in a distorted font appear on the screen: "Fox Pictures and

Regency Enterprises Present." In these few seconds the film acknowledges a tension between launching into its form and launching into its economic conditions, and that tension gets stylized as the scratch. Immediately, in its first few seconds, the film points to a contradiction between its independent aesthetic form and its industrial production. As the credit sequence proceeds, the factual information of the names of companies and laboring individuals is presented superimposed atop a morphing background of animated material in blue and black tones, which starts as just texture and then comes into greater relief as shape and finally as structure. Each name is dissolved or swallowed into the emergent animation before the next appears. Pulses of light emit between the elements of the animated structure, and the point of view travels through the structure, which looks at times like soft cells and at others like hard metal poles.

At the 1:28 mark, the structure zooms out to become an image of a pore, then further out to moisture beads and hair follicles on flesh. As the image becomes more representational, two last credits are shown, the camera zooming out from the skin to a face, and then to some indeterminate metal texture, and then more contour of the metal object, which has two holes that almost look like eyes, and then above those metal eyes, a pair of human eyes appears, wearing a scared expression, ensconced in a brow dropping with sweat, and a voice-over begins: "People are always asking me if I know Tyler Durden."

We will come back to this opening question of acquaintance and identity eventually (and to its form as a voice-over) but let us first pick up the opening sequence's interplay of the formal and the economic. This particular film instructs us that such interplay is complicated, and that being on one side or the other involves crossing the scratch. If we begin an analysis of this particular film by listing its economic details, we are following the film's own lead in rolling credits before commencing the film's form or story. However, the film itself presents that lead as a scratch, a jump, a lurch, a change in tonal registers. I will begin then, now that I have already begun, with a similar move, a one sentence description of the film followed by a Marxist version of its credits.

Fight Club is a largely successful 1999 feature fictional film directed by David Fincher that uses interesting formal techniques and a climactic twist to present the emergence and development of a somewhat anti-capitalist group political project led by an alienated white male white-collar worker. The "somewhat" anti-capitalist arguments in the film's plot reflect the ambivalence of its wholly capitalist production. Some key components of the economic base for the film include: the production budget was approximately $63 million including $17.5 million in compensation for Pitt and $2.5 million for Norton and $10,000 for Palahniuk for rights to the 1996 novel (which had sold only 5000 copies). The chain from novel to screenplay to film is an important feature of its production, highlighting multiple media, multiple types of expertise, and multi-party collaboration. Also important is the small cost for the novel and screenplay (by first-timer Jim Uhls) compared to the high cost for the superstar Brad Pitt, the lesser star Edward Norton, and then for other cast members like Jared Leto, Meat Loaf, and Helena Bonham Carter. *Fight Club*'s 139 minutes were filmed in Los Angeles with spherical lenses (an untraditional choice, lending a grainy look) on 1500 reels of film (three times the average for a 120-minute film), necessitating laborious and ingenious editing, with skyrocketing postproduction costs. After the $63 million in production costs, the film had an $11 million #1 opening weekend and at the time of this writing in 2018, it has a cumulative worldwide gross of almost $101 million, meaning that the net profits are $38 million, recouped mostly to Fox 2000 Pictures, the boutique wing of 20th Century Fox, which is #109 on the Fortune 500 List.

Although $38 million is a lot of money, the return on the investment in this case is proportionately small for the big business of Hollywood, which traffics in sums so astronomical as to be unthinkable to the majority of workers in the world. The small profits reportedly resulted in the resignation in June

2000 of the studio head Bill Mechanic, even though he had presided over Fox's ascendance to the most profitable movie company worldwide, partly through the success of *Titanic*, the first film to gross $1 billion. One producer of the film recounts in his memoir that the 20th Century Fox executives reacted to their first screening of the film "flopping around like acid-crazed carp wondering how such a thing could even have happened."[1] The head producer Laura Ziskin clashed repeatedly with Fincher about jokes and political statements and product placement in the film, and studio dislike of the film resulted in dismissing Fincher's own marketing campaign, replacing it with a more narrow promotion as a boxing movie intended for a young macho set. "It was sold as, hey come see people beat each other up," David Fincher complained to *The New York Times*, noting that the trailer was aired during wrestling matches. After this three-month marketing delay, and the fraught campaign that arguably sabotaged the box office takings, the film was released on October 15, 1999.

Fight Club met with extremely mixed reviews, with heralds ranging from "extraordinarily subversive" to "an apology for fascism"—an extremity that bespeaks the film's disclosure of ideology. The film garnered one Oscar nomination (Best Sound Editing), which suggests its technical achievements were recognized widely within its industry, even though that Oscar ultimately went to *The Matrix*. Along with *The Matrix*, *Fight Club* belonged to a great cohort of 1999 films experimenting with form through editing and CGI, including *Magnolia* and *Being John Malkovich*. Fincher was one of the first directors to work extensively on the film-DVD transition, and the resulting two-disc edition with commentary, deleted scenes, the original trailers, and more won the Online Film Critics Society Award for Best DVD. More than six million DVD copies sold between 2000 and 2010, and another seven million have sold since 2010, making it one of Fox's largest selling home-media items ever; it was released on DVD shortly after bombing in the theater, but sold so well that it was re-released in a new Blu-ray format for its tenth anniversary. The magazine *Entertainment*

Weekly gave the film a terrible grade of "D" when it premiered in theaters, but the same magazine nonetheless went on to rank the DVD as "#1" on its list of Top 50 DVDs of all time.

For a Marxist, these facts of production and consumption, of technological and historical developments, do not explain the film's ideas. But they contextualize its formal innovations and its political messages, and they point to its contradictions. The film has a deeply anti-commercial theme, indicting the emptiness of the consumerist lifestyle peddled by corporate brands like IKEA and Starbucks (Fincher famously quipped that there is Starbucks coffee cup visible in every scene), yet it was produced by a major studio using an established director (both *Seven* and *The Game* had been huge successes) and prominent stars, and in many ways its simple purpose was to make money. That it, relatively speaking, failed at this purpose is partly a result of the conflicts over how to market it, the studio's incorrect diagnosis that it would not have wide appeal, the ambivalent story the film tells, and transformations in the film industry at the time of its circulation (the rise of DVDs and decline of theater viewing). David Fincher's previous commercial successes may have enabled the risk to produce an unusual kind of film and Brad Pitt's cultural capital as a star lent the film credibility, and perhaps most decisively, the largesse of the 1990s might have licensed the freedom to think through capitalist promises. Ultimately these facts are salient because they remind us, in the Marxist tradition of assessing the connections between ideas and the relations of power in which they are articulated, that to commercialize anti-commercialism and to market anti-capitalism are contradictory endeavors. As an early review in the Associated Press reveals, these contradictions can be downright bewildering: "The movie is not only anti-capitalism but anti-society, and, indeed, anti-god . . . cause to wonder if Rupert Murdoch's company, 20th Century Fox, knew what it was doing . . . there are ideas in the film I never believed a responsible Hollywood corporation would permit to be voiced as popular entertainment."[2] To surpass such head-shaking, we must therefore attend to how

Fight Club works to activate contradictions, to illustrate them, and whether it poses resolutions to them.

As the long tail of DVD sales suggests, *Fight Club* has resonated with audiences over quite some time. This resonance is one dynamic being named when it is referred to as a "cult film," which happens frequently. *Fight Club* landed spot 16 on *Rolling Stone*'s Readers' Poll of the 25 Best Cult Movies of All Time (the number 1 spot went, unsurprisingly, to *Rocky Horror Picture Show*), and upon its ten-year anniversary *The New York Times* deemed it "surely the defining cult movie of our time."[3] A film attracts the designation "cult" when aspects of its production and consumption are irregular. This includes the financing and distribution of the film, audience reactions, and the style of the film itself. Cult films provoke controversy while simultaneously inspiring unusually devoted audiences to consume the film repeatedly. More specifically we can say that the term is used to name a certain distance from the mainstream, a certain rebellion against the conventions of the cinema of its moment. Stylistically, cult films are often bad, corny, allegorical, avant-garde, innovative, and open-ended. They are often consumed less at the theater and more on video/DVD, have reputations independent of the official reviews in the mainstream media or the awards industry, enjoy long-lasting significance, and can beget active fan cultures including imaginative responsiveness to open-endedness and ritual engagements (like dressing up for informal showings). On the production side, there may be mismatches between how a film is marketed and what audiences like about it, between what a director or actor is usually known for and how a film departs from that, between major production studios and independent houses, between how a film starts and how it proceeds.

When *Fight Club* is described this way, part of what is being marked is that people who saw the film almost instantly created venues to emulate the club. "Real" fight clubs were reported in numerous cities in California, as well as in New York and Arlington, Texas. But the designation "cult" also marks that the film has become a recurrent reference in popular culture and journalism. "The first rule of fight club is you do not talk about fight club" quickly became a ubiquitous catchphrase and remains in strong currency. With no evident occasion, in 2008 AV/Club inducted the film into its Cult Canon, in 2014 Buzzfeed published "25 Things You Didn't Know About The Movie Fight Club," and the *Huffington Post* ran a piece in 2017 titled "5 Fight Club Fan Theories That Still Make Your Head Spin 15 Years Later." It has become so available as an explanatory reference that in 2018 *The New York Times* ran an article with the headline "Inside Steve Bannon's 'Fight Club'" and in 2016 Harper Collins published a book *Feminist Fight Club: An Office Survival Manual (For a Sexist Workplace)*. *Saturday Night Live* has spoofed female fight club, and the author Chuck Palahniuk has made parody "child friendly" versions of his book. Lawyers, professors, service workers, and stay-at-home moms all regularly contribute to the twitter hashtag #fightclub, invoking the film to name quotidian conflicts and massive social contradictions alike.

But what else is being marked by calling *Fight Club* a cult film is that consumption can transform how we think about the essence of a thing. The Marxist concern with economic relations encompasses how things are produced, but also how they are consumed. Just as a commodity can be produced for one purpose but popularly used for another—Play-Doh, for instance, was on the market for twenty years as a wallpaper cleaning product before being rebranded as a toy—a film can be produced for profit but acquire cult status, thereby becoming a tactic of popular meaning-making, a map of social struggle, a prop for new affiliations. The fact that *Fight Club* reportedly inspired groups of men to set up underground boxing events but did not in the same way inspire collective housing or coordinated anti-corporate activity might give inflection to how we interpret the film's accent. At the same time, the continually renewed consumption of the film in new contexts points to *Fight Club*'s complexity, its contradictoriness, its ability to powerfully resonate long after the 1990s.

Fight Club is an exceptionally useful text with which to explore the Marxist concepts we introduced in Chapter 1—the mode of production, ideology, and mediation—because it so vividly and pedagogically engages with economic relations, ideological distortion, and opportunities for transformation. At the same time, it is a very typical film in terms of the conditions of its production, its marketing, and its popularity. It will be the thesis of this chapter that *Fight Club* comprehensively mediates the contradictory capitalist mode of production, achieving a Marxist theoretical practice of its own. *Fight Club* theorizes contradictions—social contradictions, economic contradictions, political contradictions, and psychic contradictions—and it effectuates its theory through drawing attention to the contradictions of cinematic form. Studying mediation in Marxist aesthetics entails thorough formalist inventorying of what the medium affords, paying attention to the dialectic of form and content. While some points in *Fight Club*'s plot cast aspersions on collective revolutionary agency and the psychic integrity of critics of capitalism in ways that have been interpreted as ultimately constituting a conservative political ideology, its form, including its interrogation of the medium of film, works to illustrate how any transformation of the mode of production so as to more adequately support the flourishing of human beings will necessitate completely different psychic and interpersonal relationships. Since film itself remains the preeminent popular medium, the ideological force par excellence, providing spectators with materials and codes for processing everyday life, these political transformations will also both require and result in transformations of the medium itself.

This is it, the beginning (again)

As *Fight Club* explores why subject positions are destabilized in the capitalist mode of production, it mobilizes every device in the book for breaking the fourth wall, hyperstylizing its editing, and making the medium of film itself conspicuously available for scrutiny. The plot follows an effort to reorganize the experience of subjectivity, collectivity, the body, and work in alternative formations against the ideological and material basis of the mode of production. These efforts, ranging from clubs to cooperatives to cells, are jointly coordinated by Tyler and the narrator, until the climactic revelation that the medium has been duping the spectator, utilizing projection to propagate the illusion that Tyler and the narrator are different people. Not just the mode of production, but subjectivity itself, including the technological mediation of subjectivity in close-ups, shot/reverse-shot, and point-of-view shots, are implicated.

The opening of *Fight Club*—the scratch, the credit sequence, the gun, and the voice-over narration—all set the film on a structural course that is not linear, but that we assume at the beginning will come around back to the origin. The Marxist interest in film form requires that we examine how *Fight Club* composes its plot. Plot is the patterning of a narrative. A narrative is not just what happened, but intimations of why what happened happened. Narrative theorists thus distinguish between "the queen died," which is a sentence, a fact, a statement, and "the queen died of boredom," which is a narrative because it includes a cause. The patterning of plot supplies the cause. In film, the plot includes not only the events in a narrative, but their patterning through editing, and the other material that embellishes the narrative through the camerawork, the set, and the sound. To tell the narrative of *Fight Club*, we could say it is about a man whose class alienation results in a dissociative personality disorder and in contradictory efforts to pursue new social and political relationships. But importantly the plot arranges these events out of chronological order, so the emphasis is on his friendship and collaboration with another man and their mobilization of other men to join them, and the personality disorder casts different light on the mobilization. Also important is that the plot omits events that spectators then infer, such as what explanation Tyler and Jack give to the other men when they invite them to move in to the house that becomes Project Mayhem's headquarters. An omission like this can have the effect of making the action seem spontaneous, as if there is an inevitable trajectory from boxing clubs to collective housing to terrorist bombing. The plot constitutes the story in this way. Similarly, *Fight Club* opens with a gun in Jack's mouth, and he tells us he will go back in time to how it all started. The great playwright Anton Chekhov had a rule about drama and guns: "One must never place a loaded rifle on the stage if it isn't going to go off. It is wrong to make promises you don't mean to keep." We are primed to know that we will return to this scene, and that there are some large-scale culminations of what starts small; spectators may experience a state of suspense as they anticipate these culminations. The asynchronous temporality—the flashing back function—prioritizes the political and group ramifications of what the early part of the film might seem to present as idiosyncratically personal. The plot in this way insists on the general significance of the individual, on the social context that is both the beginning and ending of the story.

Conventional Hollywood narratives center on individuals as they take actions. The star system promotes this convention, but it is also an age-old convention of protagonicity, telling the story of individual actions, exploring some characters in depth and others only superficially, as backdrops for that depth. Film as a medium is not bound to these Hollywood conventions. Specifically, because film is an art of capturing space and time, one could imagine films that meditated upon social context as the agential force by, say, setting a camera up at an intersection of two streets, prioritizing setting over character. The politics of a film might importantly turn on how agency is accorded, whether the social field is shown to determine individual actions. *Fight Club*'s flashback structure prioritizes the outcome of collective efforts, and its stunning final CGI sequence, which reportedly took almost a year to engineer, aesthetically elevates this culmination of collective struggle.

Where does collective action come from? The narrator (Edward Norton) highlights the difficulty with how to arrange his own story, which becomes the film's difficulty with how to build its plot, by saying "And suddenly I realize that all of this: the gun, the bombs, the revolution . . . has got something to do with a girl named Marla Singer." But then he has to repeatedly correct his account of origins, saying "No Wait. Back Up. Let me start earlier." On the one hand, the opening sets us up to expect events to somehow culminate in a revolutionary plot to blow up buildings, in a gunfight between two characters, and in explanatory narrative. Indeed, when the film finally returns to this beginning at its ending, there is a prolonged fadeout from an earlier scene, and then the same shot with which the film begins (the narrator blinking, with a gun in his mouth), and Tyler saying "This is it. The beginning." The double meaning of "the beginning"—both the beginning of Project Mayhem's next phase and the beginning of the film's narrative—charge this temporal ordering with complexity and call our attention to it. The film makes a winking joke of our expectation of narrative closure, a liar's paradox of "this is it. The beginning" being used to signal that this is it, the end. The narrator chimes in on the voice-over "I think this is about where we came in." On the other hand, the narrator's tone is erratic—"with a gun barrel between your teeth, you speak only in vowels" is the second line of his voice-over narration, and it is funny, a joke amid his dire situation. Who has that sense of humor? Who has the prepossession to joke while fighting for their life? Is this guy nuts? (Let me mark at this point in our analysis as well that I've started to refer to Edward Norton's character as "the narrator," but will soon stop doing this, since Brad Pitt's character also narrates, and since Edward Norton's character refers to himself as "Jack." Most of my analysis below will therefore use "Jack" but I will also return to this question of the unnamed.)

Whatever appraisals of the narrator's reliability may be, the structure of the opening orients us into a framework for meaning in which the present can only be understood with reference to the past. The patterning of the plot thus instantiates a certain Marxist materialist way of looking at things: if you want to understand where you are, you have to understand how you got there. What contingent processes in the past made the present what it is? Don't take the present as self-evident or self-justifying, and certainly don't take it as natural or inevitable.

With just its opening sequence, then, the film raises a number of questions—about form and finance, about linearity and historical consciousness, about identity and conflict. *Fight Club* is such a cinematic achievement because it uses film form to pose questions that are intensely important under the capitalist mode of production. It works as its own handbook for Marxist cultural analysis, even if it proliferates questions more than it synthesizes coherent answers. To help perceive these many questions in a relatively organized way, I suggest exploring the film's own depiction and theorization of the major concepts for Marxist film theory we laid out in Chapter 1: the mode of production, ideology, and mediation. In other words, rather than using these Marxist key concepts to analyze *Fight Club*, my argument proceeds by carefully tracking the film's own Marxist analysis. This is also the benefit of the Bloomsbury Film Theory in Practice series: by combining overviews of film theory with analyses of particular films, the series format avoids the pitfalls of theory books that undervalue film form, and of film analyses that are undertheorized. According theoretical agency to the film is an exercise in dialectics; it is also an exemplary foregrounding of mediation, Marxism's most important contribution to aesthetic theory.

Mode of production in *Fight Club*

How can a film represent or mediate the capitalist mode of production? Marxist film analysis has often broken this question down into more component parts, such as class and labor, and has often pursued the question of whether class struggle shows up within individual films. Are there working class characters? Is class division part of the plot? Is the setting expansive in ways that acknowledge the social stratification of pro-filmic space? It can also address the direct participation of divergent classes in film production. Were the male and female stars compensated equally? Were unknowns cast alongside stars? Was the film made using union and guild labor? Was the budget large or small, and who invested? The discussion below considers these usual points of Marxist analysis, but it also argues for a more expanded inquiry into film's ability to theorize production.

In the case of *Fight Club*, this conventional analysis would compel us to point out how the film depicts class struggle. As both club members and antagonists, the film includes workers in white-collar jobs, managers in white-collar jobs, blue-collar workers (bus drivers, security guards, and even police officers), and workers in the service economy (including waiters, dry cleaners, film projectionists). We see the automobile industry, the insurance industry, the airline industry, the restaurant industry, and the financial industry. We see bourgeois high-rise residences with perfectly furnished individual cells, and abandoned, ruined, old houses capable of accommodating large collectives. Moreover, beyond these direct depictions, the narrator speaks to the spectator and orients them to class relations, with exposition of worker alienation, of the evil banalities of corporate life, of the ways the growth of the service economy seems like a feminization of labor. The plot of course moves from one alienated white-collar worker's sense of his problems as psychological (insomnia, loneliness) to plural workers in disparate industries around the country buying in to something structurally lacking in their experience, to coordinated movements to transform society that include cooperative domestic labor of social reproduction (cooking and cleaning and maintaining households), integrated white- and blue-collar labor of large-scale organizational logistics and communications, and a project to destabilize the capitalist status quo and dismantle the financial economy.

But Marxist film analysis can do more than query these direct representations, this class content. It can also consider the ways films mediate social contradictions, the ways films contribute to the ability to think about contradictions. Always holding an eye on the horizon of the future, Marxist film analysis can also focus on how films estrange us from the dominant order, how they function as catalysts for social change, how they represent not existing capitalist class struggle but alternative social relations, how this energy of creating deeply realized fictional worlds is itself essential to the process of reconfiguring the given world.

Fight Club takes an interest in the capitalist mode of production through many of its motifs. The characters in the film participate in a remarkable variety of economic activities. The white-collar corporate sector is presented as deeply corrupt and hollow, nakedly calculating the limits to the value of human life. Jack explains "My job was to apply the formula. It's simple arithmetic."

> A new car built by my company leaves Boston traveling at 60 miles per hour. The rear differential locks up. . . . The car crashes and burns with everyone trapped inside. Now: do we initiate a recall? You take the number of vehicles in the field A, and multiply it by the probable rate of failure B, multiply the result by the average out-of-court settlement C. A times B times C equal X. If X is less than the cost of a recall, we don't do one.

The gruesomeness of the formula is matched only by the gruesomeness of the diegetic scene the narration overlays, in which a fellow inspector is pointing out remnants of the accident in a burned-out vehicle shell ("the teenager's braces locked around the backseat ashtray. Kinda makes a good anti-smoking ad . . . the father must have been enormous. See how the fat burned into the driver's seat, mixed with the dye of his shirt? Kinda like modern art.") In this sequence as in others, Jack's situation in the grotesquely calculative and fluorescently hollow white-collar corporate world is presented as the root cause of his psychic duress, including insomnia, dissociation, and loneliness. The other white-collar professionals he encounters, like doctors, are presented as patronizing and judgmental. The credit card industry stands for much that is objectionable under capitalism as Project Mayhem articulates it, and thus becomes slated for destruction in the bombing campaign.

The service industry is presented as peopled with intelligent, diligent, struggling people with great commonalities. Certain industries are important in the course of the film's action: the airline industry provides what Jack calls "single-serving friends" (friendships lasting the duration of a single flight, packaged like individual condiments), it provides the occasion for Jack to meet Tyler, and it provides the first words Jack speaks upon learning his own identity ("Please return your seatbacks to their full upright and locked position" he says after a man tells him he is Tyler; "we have just lost cabin pressure" he says a few minutes later when Marla confirms the same). The blue-collar professionals in government, policing, and security are portrayed ambivalently, encompassing both enemies of Project Mayhem (the police commissioner; the cop who kills Bob) and allies (detectives who won't allow Jack to expose the bomb plot; security guards who ensure no innocents will perish in the bomb plot). The retail industry provides Jack with an impoverished vocabulary for self-expression. The restaurant industry enables Jack and Tyler to spend time together socially and serves as a galvanizing target for Project Mayhem's campaign to destroy corporate franchises. Tyler explicitly identifies the service economy as the main sector from which the alienated come. He says, "The people you are after are the people you depend on. We cook your meals, we haul your trash, we connect your calls, we drive your ambulances, we guard you while you sleep. Do not fuck with us." He does so in a scene where he speaks to the commissioner of police, whom a crew of waiters working a city banquet have bound and gagged, instructing the commissioner to call off his investigation into Project Mayhem. But the camera holds Brad Pitt looking directly into it, repeating the function of hailing the audience as with other fourth wall breaks, but this time hailing a different class constituency among the spectators.

The numerous references to the film industry in *Fight Club* also contribute to its portrait of the mode of production. Tyler works as a projectionist, and we will circle back to this plot point in our discussion of the film's forms of splicing. For now, let us note that references to the film industry recur throughout *Fight Club*, and that the prominence of this industry is logically hit home by the vivid deployment of productive techniques specific to the film industry at the film's climax (the revelation that Tyler and Jack are the same).

This sheer range of industries that the film trains its sights on is useful because it contributes to economic literacy, and to economic periodization: the film explicitly locates itself at the conjuncture of airline deregulation, the rise of the service economy, the exponential expansion of credit cards, and de-industrialization. Coupled with the fact that the major creative figures in the making of the film—Palahniuk, Fincher, Pitt, Norton—were all born in the early 1960s, this periodizing energy provides something like a cognitive map of the historical and economic trappings of the story the film tells.

But more than just offering a pedagogy of economic domains, the film's industrial imagery becomes the site of its political vision when Project Mayhem starts to organize itself as a factory. "Applicants" undergo an endurance ritual to become accepted to the house; the first shot of their activities depicts three men working in the yard, raking and shoveling. The scene is filmed from inside the house, through a wall of windows with many panes, a visual that suggests the segmenting of their activities (each man in a different pane) at the same time as it calls to mind the storyboards and individual panels that make up a film. Tyler's voice-over begins, but oddly filtered as though through a PA system: "Listen up maggots. You are not special. You are not a beautiful or unique snowflake." The camera slides to the right and reveals that Tyler is speaking through a megaphone, standing outside with the workers. "You are the same decaying organic matter as everything else." Jack's voice-over takes over: "Tyler built himself an army." But the scene on screen isn't military activity; it is intensely domestic: Meat Loaf and Jared Leto in the kitchen of the house, using a dustpan and broom, wearing rubber gloves, scrubbing the stove.

Feminized economies

The domestic is an important component of Project Mayhem, the work of keeping house a necessary substrate for group undertakings. Feminist critics have seized on the gender politics in the film as a reactionary response to the feminization of labor: through the rise of the service economy, men have been feminized, and they rebel through the macho means of boxing. But as these sequences reveal, the film's story actually tells something different: in order to transform the mode of production, it is necessary to undo the gendered division of labor—to *further feminize* the work that men do. As the project develops, men move through the house carrying grocery bags, and they work in the garden and the greenhouse they've built, growing food. They work in efficient coordination at assembly-line soap production spread throughout the kitchen. Jack's narration calls it "cooking and working and sleeping in teams," and refers to the people as the "Paper Street Soap Company." It is a company that makes a domestic product *for* cleaning, *through* cooking, and *from* the surplus of social reproduction (liposuctioned fat).

   To track the film's representation of the problem of feminized labor, we need to carefully attend to the disjunction between dialogue spoken by characters and the logic of the film itself. One of the lines that feminists have cited as evidence of the film's misogyny must be interpreted in the light of the overall scene in which it is spoken and sequence in which it transpires.

Jack and Tyler are in the bathroom of the Paper St house. Jack
sits on the floor, Tyler soaks in the tub; Jack daubs at various
wounds with hydrogen peroxide, Tyler drapes a washcloth
over his eyes. They are shot in the same frame (in shallow focus
and heavy shadowing) and in reverse shots, though both are
looking straight ahead throughout, and the sound is quiet, the
tone intimate. Tyler says, "My dad never went to college, so
it was really important that I go." The generational difference
between a time when a majority of Americans did not go to
college and when a majority do is marked here, but the father's
guidance is impugned as Tyler continues "So I graduate, I call
him up long distance, and said 'Dad, now what' and he says,
'get a job.' Now I'm 25 and I call again, and say, 'Dad, now
what' and he says, 'I don't know, get married.'" Jack retorts "I
can't get married. I'm a 30-year-old boy" and Tyler speaks one
of the more famous lines in the film: "We're a generation of men
raised by women. I'm wondering if another woman is really the
answer we need." As he speaks, he turns his head toward Jack,
and Jack toward him. Slow beating music commences and
the film cuts to the kitchen, rare daylight streaming through
a curtained window, the two men together in their formal
work clothes, Jack delicately brewing coffee with primitive
instruments, pausing to straighten Tyler's tie. Jack's narration
picks up: "Most of the week we were Ozzie and Harriet" and
the camera frames him, unusually well-lit, moving through
the kitchen, whistling. Again, the logic is that the solution to
the politico-sexual dilemmas of agency the film addresses is
not less but more feminization, more domesticity. And at the
same time, this disjunction between dialogue and action recalls
the Althusserian/Žižekian definition of ideology: ideology is
not what we believe or say, but what we *do*. There may be
some disparaging dialogue about feminization, but the actions
explore the importance of domesticity and feminized labor.

The feminization question seems especially central to *Fight
Club* and stands at the center of its ability to theorize the
capitalist mode of production. Critics have more commonly
studied its gender politics than its class politics, frequently

arguing that the film ultimately investigates a crisis in masculinity in the wake of the declining industrial economy. After the 1970s, advances in factory technology and changes in international trade law precipitated a dramatic diminishment of the manufacturing economy in the United States. In its place, consumer society created many new avenues for labor, such as more restaurants, and more variety of personal services (salons, spas, gyms, coaches, consultants, tutors). Because these expanding sectors coincide so much with duties of self-care and quotidian social reproduction, sociologists have often thought of the rise of the service economy as entailing a "feminization" of labor. *Fight Club*'s constituency of waiters and baristas seem to belong to this sector, and the film's description of a male struggle to feel efficacious and engaged seems to be a correlate of participating in this sector of the economy. As Tyler puts it:

> I see in fight club the strongest and smartest men that have ever lived. I see all this potential. And I see it squandered. Goddamn it an entire generation pumping gas, waiting tables, slaves in white collars. Advertising has us chasing cars and clothes, working jobs we hate so we can buy shit we don't need. The middle children of history men, no purpose or place. We have no great war, no great depression. Our great war is a spiritual war, our great depression is our lives.

There is a direct line in this speech between the commercial and service economies and the prominence of affect over action. Lacking arenas of forceful production, the men in Generation X have only feelings, aligning them with the feminine side of an age-old gender binary of reason and emotion, external action and internal passion. Moreover, its characterization of physical activity as rejuvenating seems to harken to hard labor, manual labor, and other kinds of corporeally taxing work—the implication being that if only men were still using their bodies on the factory floor, they would not have the psychic symptoms of insomnia and alienation that Jack suffers.

A pivotal moment in the film's portrayal of feminization is also one of its most formally innovative (we will discuss the form in the mediation section). Jack is at home, sitting on the toilet, talking on the phone, and flipping through magazines. He holds one out vertically in the fashion of examining a centerfold, but the magazine isn't Playboy—it is IKEA. Since the beginnings of the widespread commercial economy in the eighteenth century, consumption has been figured as female. *Fight Club* takes this trope of the feminine consumer and represents it as the acme of male labor: men in the post-industrial economy work soulless jobs so that they can find their souls in shopping. It is also pitched as a widespread generational problem, not as an individual idiosyncrasy: "Like so many others, I had become a slave to the IKEA nesting instinct." Feminization is explicitly thematized here as the result of the growth of the consumerist, credit card driven economy.

Feminization becomes a motif in the film in the very first scene in the post-opening diegesis after the narrator's switch back. Indeed, the second line spoken by a character within this originating past is "We're still men" and it is spoken by an openly weeping man who has been introduced by the narrator only as "Bob had bitch tits." The sequence has also captured, as part of the set, a temporary sign with the words "Remaining Men Together," establishing the setting as some kind of group meeting. The voice-over says "This was a support group for men with testicular cancer. The big moosie slobbering all over me was Bob." But far from diminishing this feminine figure, the film elevates him: connecting to Bob enables Jack to sleep for the first time in months, and this connection is sustained across fight club, across Bob becoming the second recruit to Project Mayhem, and after Bob's death. The feminization that enables the intimacy between the men anchors the film's evaluations of the political projects it depicts, since it is Jack's abiding connection to Bob which prompts his own distancing from Project Mayhem, in turn prompting his discovery of his dissociated identity.

With its emphasis on the positive dimensions of feminization, the film underscores the centrality of social reproduction for any mode of production. Together with its distance from the corporate-driven capitalist mode, this enables it to probe other possibilities. The film illustrates that there are other possible modes of production both in its laments against the capitalist mode and in its evocations of other modes. Tyler's last on-screen words before the big reveal are another of his direct speeches to the audience, using the second person to project a future of ambiguous tenor.

> In the world I see you are stalking elk through the damp canyon forests around the ruins of Rockefeller Center. You'll wear leather clothes that will last you the rest of your life. You'll climb the wrist-thick kudzu vines that wrap the Sears Tower. And when you look down, you'll see tiny figures pounding corn, laying stripes of venison on the empty car pool lane of some abandoned superhighway.

Importantly, this vision is not represented on screen, relativizing it as particular and uncertain speculation. Tyler's sense of the political-economic future is primitivist, a return to capitalist prehistory, when humans made their own food and clothes and had no use for commodities, skyscrapers, superhighways. The primitivism echoes his dramatic line of questioning of Jack in their first deliberate social interaction, at the bar after the explosion at Jack's condo, when Tyler asks, "Do you know what a duvet is? Why do guys like you and I know what a duvet is? Is it essential to our survival, in the hunter-gatherer sense of the word? No." Tyler's critique of consumer society is yoked to a romanticism of pre-capitalist modes of production, a romanticism we have seen Marx did not share. There is no freedom in a return to tribal or feudal modes of production; freedom consists in a mode of production yet to come. But this moment of primitivism does not authorize reading the film as a call for a return to a time of clearer patriarchal structures;

the film grants too much respect to social reproduction in too many of its other formal elements. Tyler's gesture doesn't offer a political roadmap so much as a speculative image that foils the consumer capitalist mode of production, introducing contrasts and contradictions to incite new imaginings.

The capitalist gothic

The film's overall aesthetic might also be understood as a site of its mediation of the mode of production. Capitalism conceals its contradictions, and Marxist theory endeavors to expose them. Capitalism propagates the appearance that its mode of production is natural and just, and Marxist theory goes behind this veil. In this way Marxism constantly effectuates a rhetoric of illuminating the dark side. Marx's writings famously employ many gothic tropes. He refers to his radical break with the discipline of political economy and his puncturing of the ideology of capitalism as a turn to "the hidden abode of production," repeatedly emphasizing that his analysis of working conditions and labor's struggle for survival requires "leav[ing] this noisy sphere where everything takes place on the surface and in full view of everyone" and instead attending to the dark undersides of bustling markets and busy stock exchanges. Where official political economists tout output numbers and profit margins, Marx looks at the dirt blended with adulterated flour, the soot on factory walls, the stains on worker hands. Where bourgeois apologists praise the shine of gold, Marx frequently reassociates wealth with the labor that generated it: "Capital comes dripping from head to toe, from every pore, with blood and dirt."[4]

Fight Club's gothic aesthetic echoes this sensibility of penetrating beneath the shiny surface of consumer commodity pleasure and corporate logo polishing, to the desperate feelings of everyday laborers, the basements beneath the bars, the dim churches where the sick and the aggrieved seek solace, the grim garages where recall coordinators callously calculate death costs, the abandoned old houses across town from the featureless condos. *Fight Club*'s extremely low lighting casts almost every scene in shadow. Its scenes are almost never shot during daylight, and almost all are indoors. Its sets are dark, ugly, decaying buildings frequently shot only in partial. Its central scenes for the club are in a basement, literalizing the metaphor of "underground boxing rings" used by the police commissioner. Its music is pulsing, thudding, industrial. Its makeup is black, blue, purple, baggy insomniac under-eyes and puffy club bruises. Its unusual spherical lenses used throughout make every image gritty, grainy, elemental. Taken together these aesthetic features add up to a gothic atmosphere, a stolen glimpse into a social underside where the sun does not shine. This darkness is the correlate of corporate saturation, commercialized everything, and the credit card economy. Bleak souls, grim futures, and hidden uglies.

The visual tonality, a composite effect of camera lens, film stock, exposure, filters, and lighting, is very important in *Fight Club*. The film is visually overwhelmingly dark. Shot with a spherical lens that contributes grainy blurring, most of the scenes achieve disorientingly low contrast among colors, and throughout the lighting is disturbingly low. This darkness contributes to the bags under the insomniac eyes, the bruises on the fighter faces, the ill-applied makeup (that Helena Bonham Carter reportedly demanded), and most of all to the shadowy appearance of the characters, whose identity questions abound. There is a gothic element to the darkness, and an industrial one—everything is an obscure basement under a bar, a dimly lit garage, a weak fluorescent workplace. The overall darkness is a complicated formal feature whose effects cannot be overlooked. It confounds any simple reading of the film as promoting the political tactics represented since everything is cast in a sinister dim. It creates distance between the spectators and the shadowy protagonists, working against some promises of first-person narration. It undermines Hollywood conventions, refusing to highlight, spotlight, and flatteringly light faces for identification. It blurs the specificity of the sets and obscures the borders of scenes, compounding the obscurity of the film's setting and prolonging the transitions between scenes.

The house where Tyler and Jack reside anchors its gothic aesthetic, and stands at the center of the film's plot. Jack calls Tyler after discovering his condo explosion, ultimately seeking a place to stay, though it takes him two pitchers of beers and he still can't quite ask for shelter. The sequence leading to the first shot of the house starts with a lingering shot of a street sign "Paper St," white against the night sky, and chain link fences on the lampless street. The first shot of the house's exterior is so dark as to make it impossible to determine whether the house is a stand-alone structure or part of a row of connected buildings. The roof line is not in the frame; we are getting a part of a residence, an indistinct construction. The film cuts to inside the house in a dark foyer looking toward a door, through which Tyler and Jack enter. While decayed, the foyer and the door still connote more grandeur than the house's exterior, a set contrast that mediates household diversities. In contrast to the dilapidated exterior, the first room next to the foyer, shown in the background and emanating light, boasts a formal chandelier, decorative molding, and a shiny golden curtain. Jack stands in the foreground and the voice-over comments "I don't know how Tyler found that house, but he said he had been there for a year. It looked like it was waiting to be torn down. Most of the windows were boarded up. There was no lock on the front door from when the police or whoever kicked it in." As he says this, the camera pans the dramatic buttresses of the foyer, creating a contrast between the beauty of the house's bones and the degradation of its current condition. "It was ready to collapse. I didn't know if he owned it or if he was squatting." Quickly the contrast between ownership and occupation is added to that between past and present, grandeur and squalor. And just as quickly these layers of economic function and economic history are linked to phases of capitalist production. "There were no neighbors, just some warehouses and a paper factory. That fart smell of steam, the hamster cage smell of wood chips." The sequence ends there, proceeding to a montage of more parking lot fights, of a black-eyed Jack nodding at his boss in the men's room, of rainy nights, connoting the lapse of time. But the logic of the house established in that sequence continues to be developed throughout the film. Houses are shelter, and they are the very heart of the mode of production: making shelter, making food, making life.

The house becomes the headquarters of Project Mayhem, which it is able to do by virtue of its size (a holdover from another era) and its isolation ("alone for a half a mile in every dimension"). The members of Project Mayhem are able to live together, treating their project as a way of life rather than an extracurricular activity, because they do not pay rent in the house. In close shots of material texture, the house's walls and beams, plumbing and lighting, wood and metal, are all lavishly detailed. Jack narrates "Nothing worked. . . . Rain trickled down through the plaster and light fixtures, everything wooden swelled and shrank, everywhere were rusted nails to snag your elbow on." The house can be squatted in because it is devalued in the cult of the glistening new, but the materials endure, and the shelter still basically provides. Later, when the house mirrors its neighbors and becomes a soap factory, its setting condenses the domestic site of social reproduction with the industrial site of commodity production. When Project Mayhem turns the house into logistics headquarters for their diverse endeavors, they install wall-hung file organizers, desks, more lighting, and bulletin boards, mimicking an office environment. At the same time, they coordinate cooking and cleaning and gardening, in a highly cooperative domestic center. The set-direction choice to use the house as setting for all of these activities creates a complex image of household economics, of many strata and phases of economic production superimposed atop one another. In this way the film uses both its story and its medium-specific rendering of space to theorize about the interconnection and coexistence of different aspects of the capitalist mode of production, beginning to differentiate between those that are particular to capitalism and those that would be part of non-capitalist production.

Creative destruction

We might not instinctually think that a mode of production also involves modes of destruction. But *Fight Club* works to theorize just how connected accumulation and destruction can be—it works to trace the contradictions of "production." The film uses several motifs of destruction, and destruction centers its most cataclysmic events—the first fight, the dissociated self, and the dynamite demolitions. We can start our analysis of these destructive tropes and their connection to Marxist theory by considering the film's conclusion, which depicts the culmination of Project Mayhem in the destruction via detonation of eight skyscrapers, the financial center of operations in any town. This culmination is one of the film's innovations beyond Palahniuk's original novel (in which Project Mayhem ultimately targets not the credit industry but the Museum of Natural History).

While the film doesn't directly specify its city, the novel is set in Wilmington, Delaware. The film contains key allusions to Wilmington. Tyler's business card, which he offers Jack in their first encounter, gives his address as Bradford, 19808; Jack's boss's business card, framed for just a moment in the pivotal self-fight scene, also lists Bradford, 198090 (the extra digit a sore-thumb betraying the falsity) and while there is no Bradford at 19808, that is the zip code for Wilmington. Furthermore, Fincher and set designers made the choice to film in Wilmington, *California*, going so far as to rent an abandoned bar and give it a new neon sign (Lou's, the crucial setting for the first drink between Tyler and Jack, their first fight, and all the initial basement sessions of the club) and to build the Paper St house there. Wilmington, De is home to 64 percent of all incorporated firms with public disclosures in the United States. This is an astounding number and doesn't come about because the corporations are physically housed or operating in Wilmington, but rather because they rent post office boxes (and/or hire lawyers) to serve as legal addresses for the chartering incorporation papers, since the state laws and court structure (a court of Chancery) are the most corporate-favorable out of any of the fifty states. Making Wilmington the target of destruction marks the Project's systematic vision, its move from bodily destruction and property destruction to a higher order of magnitude: the destruction of the credit economy.

What is profound about this target, and what the film's open-ended conclusion underlines, is that the credit economy is already itself based on widespread destruction: on the indebting of individuals who subsist in a system that privatizes elementary goods and services for profit, that denigrates public and collective resource management, that transfers the burdens of sustaining life from the aggregate to the individual. Economic historians, economists, and sociologists have repeatedly evidenced that the popularization of credit card usage and astronomical growth of consumer debt coincides historically with the stagnation of wages in the United States after the early 1970s. Household debt relative to GDP has steadily increased since the 1950s; while it amounted to only 24 percent of GDP in the 1950s, it hovers around 78 percent in the 2010s. Credit card debt is only one component of household debt (mortgages, auto loans, and student loans are the other three) but it is the most negative: both houses and college degrees should provide some return on their debt in the form of new equity, new access to higher wages, etc., and auto loans provide the use of access to work (since there is egregiously little public transit in the United States). This historically specific ballooning of consumer debt should not be contrasted with an earlier, less credit-oriented stage of capitalism, since all capital is essentially credit: the suspension of disbelief in the concept of value. In destroying the destruction, the Project enables spectators to perceive the credit economy as destructive, and to perceive some destruction as generative. As they put it, "if we erase the debt record, then we all go back to zero." The film's chronological structure reinforces the strategic focus in which the plot culminates and which the last shot showcases: the destruction at the end is only the beginning, since the film takes the destruction for its own beginning.

Although it might appear otherwise, destruction lies at the heart of the capitalist mode of production. Primitive accumulation, accumulation by dispossession, and imperial colonization are all formations of destroying what is held commonly, publicly, or for use, and turning it to private account. Environmental destruction is absolutely constitutive of capitalist extraction, capitalist over-production, and the carbon economy. Planned disasters like privatized infrastructure, unaddressed climate change, and international debt default are each catastrophes that provide capitalism with new occasions for accumulation. *Fight Club* doesn't probe all these historical and spatial levels of destruction, but in elevating destruction as a trope it mediates them.

The film offers other types of destruction for consideration, since beyond highlighting the corporate economy's production through destruction, and beyond the strategy to destroy the credit card industry, Project Mayhem uses destruction as a tactic. The project coordinates numerous acts of destruction, like demagnetizing all the VHS movies at Blockbuster Video, committing vandalism against late model expensive cars, trashing chain coffee bars, and ruining corporate public art displays. The individual applicants to Project Mayhem commit a certain destruction of their daily lives since they presumably resign their jobs and liquidate their households to sign up, as they can bring only three changes of clothing, no personal possessions, and $300 personal burial money. They also undergo a bodily and emotional deprivation test, standing unmoving, unfed, unencouraged, unsheltered outside the Paper St house for seventy-two hours as initiation rite, and eventually shaving their heads, dressing only in black. But far and away the most important destruction, central to the way the film is able to theorize social transformation, is self-destruction.

"Self-improvement is masturbation. Now, self-destruction . . . ." Tyler doesn't finish the sentence, spoken as he peruses banner ads for gyms and education on a crowded subway train, but the implied ending might be some contrast with masturbation like "sexual intercourse," or "collective orgy," or "total abstinence." This erotic charge behind the idea of self-destruction is a titillating clue to how the film thinks about selfhood; after self-destruction, there remains erotic energy and dynamic animation. This is why fight club grows so magnetically and also why it evolves: the bodily harm strikes at the image-basis of commodity society, at the false selfhood peddled in IKEA catalogues and wellness centers, activating a different source of selfhood, a libidinally charged propulsion.

The film's apotheosis of self-destruction unfolds in the contradiction it stages between Jack's self and Tyler's self. When they are revealed to be two different personas in the same person, rather than two men in a relationship with each other, it becomes evident that what is generally considered the normal function of the ego is not in effect. Jack's self has come undone. The medical literature on dissociative disorder generally holds that individuals develop alternate personalities in order to cope with personal traumas. Brilliantly, *Fight Club* resists this expert wisdom, framing alternate personalities as techniques for coping with *social* traumas. *Fight Club* presents Tyler as an alternate personality for Jack as he copes with the personal symptoms—insomnia and numbness—of social traumas of alienation, meaninglessness, the logic of surplus accumulation, and the contradictions of capitalism. Jack's personality disorder reflects not some individual trauma like an abusive childhood, but the diffuse systemic catastrophe of working for the insurance industry, with its grotesquely calculating approach to human life, and working toward the rewards of accumulating stuff. At the great reveal, Tyler lays out their shared identity in very interesting terms: "All the ways you wish you could be, that's me. I look like you wanna look, I fuck like you wanna fuck, I am smart, capable, and most importantly, I am free in all the ways that you are not." He suggests that he is not only a compensatory personality, but an ego-ideal, a fulfillment of Jack's ambitions for the way he wants to be seen. Tyler starts with looks, bringing home the connection between image culture and available vocabularies for selfhood: we define ourselves as images; selfhood is a moving image, a film we play for ourselves and for others. We see ourselves being seen.

Film as a medium can show us that the economic mode of production also works as a psychological mode of production—that our selves and psyches are just as much products as are commodities and profits. *Fight Club* makes this observation into a theory of the radicalization of the subject: any change in the mode of production must also be a change in the mode of subjectivization. And, as the film shows, this entwining means that revolutionary economic transformation is circuitous and recursive, mutually activated with and by psychic reconfigurations. Theorists such as Julia Kristeva and Gilles Deleuze have long argued that dissociations can be thought of as a political practice, an activity of dissenting from the common sense of dominant ideology and the hegemonic arrangements of psychic life to support politically contingent relations like the capitalist mode of production. *Fight Club* contributes to this tradition, effectively floating the thesis that psychic self-destruction is integral to politico-economic revolution. The self-destruction in *Fight Club* dramatizes, as Slavoj Žižek argues, that "we cannot go directly from capitalist to revolutionary subjectivity: the abstraction, the foreclosure of others, the blindness to the other's suffering and pain, has first to be broken . . . (a break) which cannot but appear extremely violent."[5]

This break is developed by one of the film's climaxes, in which the narrator fights himself, but in the guise of fighting his boss. Self-destruction is brilliantly rendered as a social act of political class war. Jack knocks at his boss's office, and by the time he leaves he has engineered an unusual exit package. The scene is better lit than most in the film, thanks to the office fluorescents, so instead of framing the faces in shadow, the camera uses profile shots to introduce a different rhetoric of partiality. "Let's pretend," he starts, carefully floating a fictional scenario in which he reports to the federal transportation regulatory agency the misdoings of the companies for whom he has calculated recalls. "You keep me on the payroll as an outside consultant and in exchange for my salary my job will be never to tell people these things that I know." The boss shouts invective and calls for security, and the narrator's fist quivers in a shallow focus shot; he punches himself repeatedly, keeping up a running commentary for overhearers as if the boss is at fault. "Oh my god! Why would you do that? No! Please stop!" The camera shows the boss's riveted, bewildered face in successive medium shots, suggesting the break in his fabric of normalcy. In the middle, there is a stop-motion frame, a little blurred, and the voice-over says, "For some reason, I thought of my first fight, with Tyler." The blurring, the freezing, and the voice-over, as well as the reflexive memory, all highlight the relation between the film's formal construction and the political act of self-destruction taking place. The prominence of images and appearances becomes crucial: a bloodied Jack kneels before the boss, detritus of office furniture everywhere, reiterating his deal: "Give me the paychecks, like I asked, and you won't ever see me again," and then breaks into the voice-over: "And right then, at our most excellent moment together" security arrives, and Jack responds "Oh thank god. Please don't hit me again." Whether because the company creates special severance for him upon the appearance of violence from his boss, or because his boss honors the deal, the beneficial exit is achieved: "We now had corporate sponsorship. This is how Tyler and I were able to have fight club every night of the week." Accounting for its own financial condition of possibility is essential for the film's representation of the capitalist mode of production; without a modicum of resources, movements will have trouble scaling up.

This sequence fabulously interweaves the question of destruction and of what destruction can create (in this case, bodily harm and financing for a political insurgency), the question of self-relation and how that transforms self-other relations (self-destruction as the vehicle for breaking with the boss and for confounding his own ideology), and the question of how appearances can become material forces (either the appearance that Jack has been beaten by his boss secures his severance, or the striking spectacle of self-destruction does). And all of these questions are refracted by the film's self-mediation in its special camerawork, unusual lighting, and voice-over.

At the film's conclusion, the motif of self-destruction and the violence entailed in the ruptures of ordinary social relations culminate in Jack shooting himself. He points the gun under his chin, apparently intending to commit suicide as a way of arresting Tyler's plans. But the plans are inexorably in motion, incorporating people nationwide, and the leader's death will make no difference. The gunshot angle proves fortuitously nonlethal, and with a wisp of blue smoke, Tyler is extinguished. Jack emerges as a new subject, activated by the scope of revolutionary destruction he has envisioned, including the destruction of shooting himself, filmed in close-up straight on, speaking in a calmer voice and acting in a more self-possessed manner than at any preceding point in the film. He looks at Marla and says, "Look at me. Everything is going to be alright." Through a synchronized act of personal destruction and coordinated political destruction, the film thematizes interlinking psychic and social transformations.

Fight Club frames itself as a reflection on the cult of images and their role in the capitalist mode of production. From Jack's indications that his alienation expresses itself as numbness to the bombardment of images and his struggle to locate an original that can arrest the phantasmagoric flow of "a copy of a copy of a copy," to Tyler's first words about the ideology of airline safety instruction cards and his first lengthy speech about the distortions of advertising, from the graffiti pranks to cornflower-blue software icons, from the importance of splicing to the intertextual allusions and the constantly blurred frame, the film explores how images work ideologically, how images interpellate subjects, how images manufacture consent, how corporate logos saturate the visual field, how Hollywood represents imaginary relations to real conditions of existence. This thoroughgoing reflection on the social power of images inflects the film's ultimate messages.

Fight Club remarkably studies the capitalist mode of production. Even as many critics have complained that one trajectory of its plot seems to undermine Marxist critique because Project Mayhem becomes too worryingly undemocratic, cultish, or even, as some have argued, fascist, the film as a whole offers much more than this element of the plot. The depiction of the mode of production in its gothic tonality, in its complex logics of feminization, in its integration of so many industries, in its reflections on the film industry, in its creative destruction contribute profoundly to the Marxist project of investigating the capitalist mode of production in order to map its contradictions and counteract its claim to be the only possible mode.

Ideology in *Fight Club*

Of course, to say that the film helps to investigate the capitalist mode of production, and thereby participates in Marxist theorizing, is not to say that the film isn't ideological. Recall that defining ideology is a point of theoretical debate, but that we can usefully understand it in the terms developed by Althusser: ideology is the representation of an imaginary relation to real conditions of existence. This representation can be grasped on the model of projection, throwing forth images that interpellate the subject and constellate the real conditions of existence into a contrived cohesiveness. In this way, projective technology like the cinema can be a privileged site for the critique of ideology since cinema can formally elaborate the means by which ideology operates. We have seen that the camera obscura, an early projective technology and precursor of photography and thus the cinema, plays a crucial role in Marx's explicit theorization of ideology. And we have seen how Marxist theorists like Adorno and Horkheimer place film at the center of their account of the industrial production of ideology. But it remains for us to explore how film is not just an example of ideological mechanisms or a commodity on the ideological marketplace but also can itself constitute a critique of ideology, by deploying its formal proximity to projection in general, and by theorizing its own medium.

Fight Club is a perfect film for this exploration because it is so interested in the formal workings of ideology. Ideology is an overt topic in the story of individuals estranged from their conditions of existence who are nonetheless hindered in their efforts to do something new by their constrained imaginations, their cathexis to a charismatic leader, and his own estrangement from himself. But beyond this, the film incorporates into its form reflections on projective technology that highlight ideological functioning. In our discussion of how the film represents the capitalist mode of production, we mentioned that the film industry itself is arrayed among the diverse strata of employment and production that *Fight Club* assembles. The film arguably accords a certain privilege to the film industry by associating it with Tyler: the brilliant, critical leader of its movement for self-destruction and collective action is also employed as a film projectionist, a technician of illusion. What is more, as we'll discuss below, he uses knowledge about the production of film to also intervene in the illusions film projects, splicing alternative images in to reels to disrupt the fictive seamlessness of the diegetic world, and to stir spectators into less complacency. In this way the film suggests that film itself is ideologically ambivalent: it is the technology of ideology, stemming from the camera and projection, but it is also a medium for the critique of ideology.

Our review of Marxist theories of ideology also encompassed the ways that ideological projections and imaginary relations can often be instantiated in the realm of practice and action. Ideology is what we do, not what we believe. "They do not know it, but they are doing it." *Fight Club* devotes itself to exploring this realm of action. Jack's professional life is the foremost example of such action. Even though Jack suffers from insomnia, loathes his boss, and finds his industry morally repugnant, he keeps calm and carries on. The film has numerous sequences of his going through the motions at work while nursing private ideas about the corruption there, and far from elevating his revolutionary sentiments, these scenes showcase the contradiction between quotidian action and critical sentiment. For example, we see Jack sitting at his desk staring into space, the voice-over relaying a grim prognosis about space—about corporate exploration of outer space: "When deep space exploitation ramps up, it will be corporations that name everything. The IBM Stellar Sphere. The Microsoft Galaxy." He is absorbed in his counter-world, telling his critical story, but he is also at work, making copies, filing claims, running calculations, and interacting with his coworkers and boss. When his boss approaches with a new assignment for him, the camera shows the boss's torso, but cuts off his head, accentuating the mindless quality of the interaction. The boss addresses Jack in a bland monotone devoid of pleasantries, and Jack replies in what the screenplay describes as "listless management-speak": "I'm going to need you out of town a little more this week. We've got some red-flags to cover." "You want me to de-prioritize my current reports until you advise of a status upgrade?" "You need to make these your primary action items." Jack carries off a professional exchange even though his mind is elsewhere. The film uses the medium difference between voice-over and diegetic speech to represent this distance, alternating the lines Jack speaks with lines he narrates: "I'm going to need you out of town a little more this week. We've got some red-flags to cover." "It must've been Tuesday. He was wearing his cornflower-blue tie." "You want me to de-prioritize my current reports until you advise of a status upgrade?" "You need to make these your primary action items." "He was full of pep. Must've had his latte enema."

The distance between the two voices marvelously illustrates the workings of ideology: it is our everyday practical action, independent of belief, our listless accession to the rules of the game—the headless manager who earnestly enjoys, the spineless worker who readily obeys—which guarantees this set of social relations will be held in place, but it is also our sense of our own distance from these actions, our carving out of a critical dimension in which our voice-over can really define us, our imagining ourselves to really exist in that dimension, positing a naïve other who doesn't. Ideology is what we do. But it is also the illusory freedom of our cynicism in doing what we do but telling ourselves we object to it. It is our shared language of interaction, and it is our spiritual notion of freedom. *Fight Club*'s ability to represent both of these levels stems directly from its staging of the contrast between the voice-over and the diegesis. It stems as well from the sound editing that plays the boss's discourse continuously under the voice-over, assembling the contradictory non-conversation. And visually it stems from the vertical axis along which the camera moves, since Jack sits at his desk, the boss stands, and their heads cannot appear in the same frame. After the headless shot, the camera looks up at the boss and down at Jack. But the voice-over, a meta-commentary from above, revises this hierarchy by introducing an abstract superiority into the spatial relationship. The material hierarchies of power and exploitation (the boss and the worker, the real conditions of existence) are represented in their imaginary version (the disaffected worker morally superior to, and hipper than, the cornflower-blue boring boss). It is ideological that the boss thinks his action items are meaningful. Yet it is also completely ideological that Jack thinks he is somehow freer, smarter, cooler because he voices objections to his boss in his mind. He continues to work—that is what he does.

The ideology of professional practice is not confined to the corporate workplace. When Jack goes to see a doctor in search of sleeping pills for his insomnia, the doctor refuses to write a prescription, saying "You need to lighten up. . . . You need healthy, natural sleep. Chew some valerian root and get more exercise." "I'm in pain." "You want to see pain? Swing by First Methodist on Tuesday nights. Testicular Cancer. That's pain." The highly educated professional class is suspicious of drug-seeking workers, and indifferent to their culturally induced insomnia and pain. Expertise can be used to impose a factual metric of comparison between bodily and spiritual suffering, between worthy and unworthy pain. In the guise of expert, fact-based conduct, values are communicated, social relations upheld. In the guise of common sense and appeals to nature, workers are pathologized. Even those individuals with enough education to theoretically fathom the contingent history of the capitalist mode of production, or the power of advertising to shape desires, blithely reproduce society at every turn.

The Marxist theory of ideology casts aspersions on those who would feign to be outside of ideology. *Fight Club* illustrates this dynamic of the knowing subject who thinks that only others believe in ideology with its strange plot strand about support groups. The unsympathetic doctor who directs Jack to the suffering of cancer patients invokes a contrast between Jack's spiritual suffering and the corporeal pain of the patients. For reasons unexplained, witnessing that intensity somehow relieves Jack's numbness, enabling him to sleep, and to continue his everyday life, for a year. Jack opines that his fellow group-goers "really, really listen" to him and "love" him. He doesn't use his own name, instead wearing nametags with different aliases for each group, and he doesn't speak. As he explains, "The less I said, the harder they cried." The groups are positioned by the story as an upgraded coping mechanism, parallel to the IKEA obsession in their function to address his emptiness, but much more successful. In arraying the two mechanisms like this, the film's narrative creates a link between consumerism and group relations, suggesting that both are realms of illusion. The illusory quality is particularly accentuated when another "tourist," another cynical knower, starts attending the group, and her distance from the illusion disturbs the narrator's closeness to the illusion. As the camera focuses closely on Marla, the Narrator says "She ruined everything. Her lie reflected my lie. So I felt nothing." After some antagonistic negotiation with Marla, the Narrator settles that they will share the groups, taking alternate evenings. The illusion can only function when the narrator pretends that the others are all believers; the presence of another knower dismantles that pretense. Ideology is something we like to attribute to others, never to ourselves.

Generalizing ideology

This ambient sense that ideology is "out there" is reinforced by the film's imprecise setting, which seems to diffuse ideology to a general realm of everyplace. *Fight Club* makes lots of broad arguments about how the economic base conditions social relations, bodily experience, and psychic well-being, and it fortifies this breath by remaining very vague about setting. The narrator is unnamed. When asked which car company he works for, he replies "a major one." The city where he resides is not directly identified nor does he have any special identification with it: "Home was a condo on the fifteenth floor of a filing cabinet for widows and young professionals." Although a "generation" is repeatedly cited, and some economic indicators included, there is no date for the events. Many characters, several played by famous actors, are important players in the film's story even though they are never given names. This indistinction is a vehicle of the film's generalizations, a way that it extends its insights across time, space, individuals. The ideas the film propounds about the interrelation of the psychic and the political-economic are ideas it wants to offer as generally illuminating, generally useful.

The unidentified setting, unidentified protagonist, and unidentified characters also reinforce the thematic exploration of troubles with identity that the film advances. As we saw in the opening scene, and as the plot twist reveals, identities are illusory. At the same time, they are materially determined by class position, economic activity and privilege, and social practices. When the film does not simply take identities as given, it calls our attention to these processes of illusion, construction, determination. And therefore makes us think of identity as a crux of social transformation. We must identify and desire and connect differently if we want the mode of production to change, and changing the mode of production will enable new patterns, categories, and expressions of identity to emerge.

Outside of the workplace, actions in the sphere of consumption also constitute ideology and reproduce the social relations of the mode of production. When Jack first meets Tyler, the film develops this idea. The third sentence Tyler speaks is "The illusion of safety," in reference to the emergency exit row instructions he is perusing on the airplane; he then asks Jack "You know why they put oxygen masks on planes?" Jack replies reflexively "So you can breathe," but Tyler shakes his head no and retorts "Oxygen gets you high. In a catastrophic emergency you are taking giant panicked breaths. Suddenly you become euphoric, docile, you accept your fate. It's all right here" and then he gestures to the instruction illustrations. "Emergency water landing, 600 miles an hour. Blank faces, calm as Hindu cows." Tyler is instantly established as a puncturer of illusions, as a keen analyst of the propagation of illusion through representations like the instructions and through ritualized habits like the verbal assent flight attendants require of passengers seated in an exit row to accept their responsibility.

Jack is charmed by Tyler's "interesting theory" and his frank talk about subjects everyone else would rather ignore. Tyler reveals just how much ideology is not a deep misguided belief, but practical consciousness, the way we act as if commercial flying is safe, the way we act as if the reason airlines supply oxygen is for health rather than for sedation, the way we are not only docile but euphoric in acceding to the everyday reality of the social contradictions of capitalism. The sequence is filmed with characteristic low lighting, resulting in heavy shadow on one side of the both actors' faces while they talk. Although both actors are captured in the same frame frequently in the sequence, the focus is shallow, so that only the man speaking is clear, while the other remains somewhat blurry. Through these cinematic techniques, the film imbues the conversation's thematic content about illusions with formal effects of shadows and opacity. Such techniques therefore implicate technologies of representation in the production of docility and in the production of new vigilance.

Fight Club captures the Althusserian theory of ideological interpellation in its representation of subjective formation in connection with the advertising and film industries. After the reveal, Norton's realization of his psychic diversity is illustrated through replaying earlier, pivotal scenes in the film, but with Brad Pitt edited out, representing to the spectator scenes they have already witnessed, but highlighting the editorial construction of those scenes. When Jack confronts Tyler about their joint identity, the editing work is paramount. "Why do people think that I'm you?" he asks, and Tyler replies "I think you know," prompting a flash to the earlier scene of threatening the police commissioner. In rapid succession, other scenes replay, but they are re-shot and re-edited to substitute Edward Norton for Brad Pitt (as in the second-person, fourth-wall break "You are the all singing all dancing crap of the world" speech) or Brad Pitt is cut out and Edward Norton is shown alone (as in the scene of the lye burn). These flashes of masterful editing laminate Jack's realizations atop the cinematic apparatus: his process of losing illusion is analogized to the process of manufacturing moving images. The film suggests in this way that our ability to know our own psychic formations is intimately entwined with the media apparatus of image production. Tyler further underscores "All the ways you wish you could be, that's me. I look like you want to look," connecting the generating of ego-ideals to the ubiquity of images in phantasmagoric celebrity culture.

As the fight club builds momentum, Jack's narrates, "It was right in everyone's face. Tyler and I just made it visible. It was on the tip of everyone's tongue. Tyler and I just gave it a name. . . . We all started seeing things differently. Everywhere we went, we were sizing things up." Ideology isn't what people know or don't know, it is what they do; the advent of fight club gives people something different to do. Instead of moving through week after week for no purpose other than accumulating money, they move through the days to get to the weekend for its exercises of destruction. Critics often interpret the film as offering physical violence as antidote to spiritual alienation: the corporeal suffering of the fight at once alleviates and concentrates the spiritual suffering of the class struggle. The alienation of the everyday is redressed with *immediacy*: the intensity of bodily pain, the nonverbal character of the social interactions (even "the first rule of Fight Club is you do not talk about Fight Club" bespeaks the intuitive, telegenic transmission of the connections), the anonymity of the fighters, their code of silence when not on the fight floor ("This kid from work, Ricky, couldn't remember whether you ordered pens with blue ink or black . . . but Ricky was a god for ten minutes when he trounced the maître d' of a local food court"). The film opens itself to this reading; I have just produced a number of plot points as evidence for it. But the problem with this reading is that plot points are only one element of film form. And *Fight Club* is a film whose other elements—mise-en-scène, lighting, performances, and more—cohesively generate, underscore, and theorize mediacy rather than immediacy.

Ideology is what we do at work. It is what we do when we consume. And it is even, *Fight Club* insists, what we do when we think we're breaking out of ideology. This contradictory status of political struggle comprises one of the film's most disturbing moments.

Members of Project Mayhem are working in the house at night, when suddenly yelling is heard in the distance, and breathless members run in, carrying a body. Explaining that they were on assignment, killing two birds with one stone—destroying a piece of corporate art and trashing a corporate coffee bar—the men reveal that one of their number has been shot in the head. The revelation is shocking because it is a different kind of hurt than the fights in the club; it is the industrialized and impersonal injury of the lethally weaponized police which incurs no obstacles to committing violence against nonviolence. Why does breaking a window warrant the use of deadly force? The body is Bob, Jack's original friend from the testicular cancer support group. Jack experiences distressed grief and pronounces "He was my friend. This is Robert Paulson," and a member interrupts "But Sir, we don't have names in Project Mayhem." Jack insists "his name was Robert Paulson" and a member of the group experiences an epiphany, announcing "In death, a member of Project Mayhem has a name. His name was Robert Paulson" and another member repeats, then another, and soon the entire room is chanting "His name was Robert Paulson." As the scene eerily illustrates, ideology is our spontaneous generation of meaning amid terrible circumstances, our introduction of concepts to dispel contradictions, and it is our presumption that what others actualize as meaning is meaningful. It is our willingness to go along with a leader, and our willingness to go along with a group. In the scene Jack wears a white shirt and appears under a bright light, while the anonymous members, dressed in black, are dimly lit, a set choice that literalizes Jack's enlightenment vis-à-vis the deluded masses. But this enlightenment is also ideological: earnest personal feeling and empathic individualizing regard for others does not transform the social relations in the capitalist mode of production. Collective actions do, but the film is, in this scene, invested in pathologizing the collective.

Yet Jack's insider-outsider status and his shrieking "you morons!" can hardly be taken as the heroic counter-ideology, especially as it soon becomes his idiosyncratic refusal of the substantive, coordinated project to change things. In what the film depicts as a futile mania, he visits cells around the country and tries to dismantle their plans, but the momentum is too effective; he calls security guards at the target buildings to warn them of the bombs and they reassure him everything is going according to plan; he turns himself in to the police and several of the detectives try to stop him. The buy-in to the bomb plan is tremendous, concerted, and seemingly nationwide. Janitors and guards and middle managers alike have arranged for the buildings to be empty. The collective action is collaborative and effective. The film uses Jack's estrangement to underscore that Project Mayhem is not unideological but rather a counter-ideology to the prevailing consumerist corporate capitalism. There is no outside of ideology; it's not a matter of the ideological bosses and the anti-ideological workers but of how to stage a clash of ideologies, and how to scale-up that clash into collective practices for social transformation.

The ultimate way the film theorizes ideology is by locating its climax at this juncture of clashing ideologies. As Jack goes on the road to undo Tyler's plans, he confronts disciplined non-response, winking acknowledgment, and confusion, which comes to a head as a bartender finally tells him "You're Tyler Durden." Jack's estrangement from Project Mayhem is at this climax revealed to be a function of his dissociative disorder; his critical distance from what he perceives as an ideology is itself exposed as a delusion. Moreover, the climax also recasts the question of the position from which anyone can conduct a critique of ideology or endeavor to articulate alternative social meanings.

We have seen Marx, Althusser, Žižek, and others insist that there can be no outside of ideology, and that precisely when someone claims to be unideological, or when a critic claims to be above ideology, that may be where ideology is most tenaciously effective. *Fight Club* operationalizes this profound position in the theory of ideology by using dissociative disorder and dramatic revelation to undermine Jack and Tyler's externality to the system they criticize. The charismatic leader who seems the most estranged from the capitalist mode of production, and the suffering worker who eagerly becomes his lieutenant, shepherding recruits all over the country from the restaurant industry to the police, are enlightened. But they are both benighted about the truths closest to them, unaware of their own subjective positions. Precisely at the point that seems most expressly outside of ideology—leading a huge movement against the capitalist mode of production, about to culminate in a world-changing political act—they are forced to confront their own delusions. The film deploys conventional expectations about the medium—that, say, one actor equals one character—as well as plot structure and narration to generate these confrontations. It makes itself into a map of contradictions.

Mediation in *Fight Club*

The Marxist idea of mediation connotes the social practice of representation—how representations represent the phenomena presenting in social life, how representation acts upon those phenomena, how representation participates in the dialectic of ideology and ideology critique. Thus far our exercise of a Marxist analysis of *Fight Club* and a Marxist theory in dialogue with *Fight Club* has been driven by the dialectical procedures of balancing context with text and particulars with wholes, and by heeding the inevitability of contradiction. In this final section on mediation, I want to wrap things up by arguing that the numerous sophisticated ways that *Fight Club* mediates the capitalist mode of production and the cinematic mode of production enable it to contribute profoundly to mapping social contradiction. The upshot of my analysis will not be a report card on whether the film passes or fails a Marxist litmus test. Rather, in keeping with the ongoing social practice of interpretation and with the techniques of situated, contradictory reading, I will argue that this film rewards careful scrutiny, making it an excellent resource with which to think about, teach, and mobilize Marxist concepts.

We have seen that *Fight Club* overtly thematizes both the capitalist mode of production and ideology. It takes these two key Marxist concepts as fodder for its dialogue, plot, and style. To consider how it takes up mediation, another key concept, let's turn to the film's form and form system. There, we will find that the film provides additional, substantive points of entry into the Marxist question of how representation acts on the world. We will also find basis for concluding our analysis, since form must always be the ultimate site of an artwork's activation of contradiction.

Fight Club achieves a mediation of the capitalist mode of production and of ideology through its form, which constellates intensely self-reflexive investigations of the medium of cinema. Mediation is communicating, making relations, middling between extremes—so thinking about medium as the vehicle of mediation is an essential first step in cinema's social practice. From the first pane to the last, *Fight Club* includes film among the technologies of producing this social order from which it dissents. It does so in small ways like breaking the fourth wall with a character looking and speaking directly into the camera, and it does so in large ways, like featuring the film editing technique of splicing as one of its plot points and central tropes. These references make the cinematic apparatus itself an object of study, enabling spectators to think about the industrial construction of reality and the superstructure of late capitalism, and to think specifically about film itself as a major element of that superstructure.

I have organized this section around six aspects of *Fight Club*'s form that constitute artistic achievements which also reflect on the medium of cinema, and which actualize the film's critical representation of the capitalist and cinematic modes of production. These six aspects are cinematographic innovations, genre-bending, intertextuality, splicing, narration, and inconclusiveness. Each of these ways in which *Fight Club* works relate the story it is telling to the technology of its telling. The film's form thus concretely exercises the Marxist practice of contextualization. Moreover, my analysis of these aspects of the form ought to exercise the importance of Marxist attention to form as the dialectical complement to its attention to context. If we merely catalogue *Fight Club*'s economic investments, it is harder to appraise the film's possible critical interventions, the ways it uses the medium of film and film form to intervene in the social relations of which it is a part. At the same time, we have to think of form in dimensions beyond the plot points we have considered so far in our discussion of the mode of production and of ideology. *Fight Club* theorizes mediation by practicing the self-reflexive presentation of the medium of cinema.

Cinematographic innovations

The filming of *Fight Club* incurred great expense to shoot triple the average number of feet of film, and scenes were often filmed from two or more cameras simultaneously, doubling the labor of camera-operation and lighting. Savvy and experimental use of CGI peppers the film. Editing is a motif in the film, and the editing costs for *Fight Club* were enormous, due to how many feet had to be processed. All of these junctures at which more-than-average labor was exerted in the making of the film culminate in some truly memorable and innovative sequences, which in turn deepen the film's mediation of the capitalist mode of production.

The most cinematographically innovative sequence in the entire film evinces critical ambivalence toward what images produce. Jack is talking on the telephone (a cordless cradled between his chin and his shoulder) while using both hands to turn a magazine 180 to behold its centerfold, but then the camera reveals that he is sitting on a toilet, and the voice-over reveals that the smut in the magazine is not bodies but commodities: "We used to read pornography. Now it was the Horchow Collection." As he speaks, the camera zooms in to the catalog page, embarking on a 360-degree pan through the space of an apartment but that quickly becomes visual acrobatics of melding the medium of the print catalog with that of film. The tracking pan is overlaid with textual graphics that simulate catalog copy: large text in the signature IKEA font depicting trademark faux-or para-Swedish names ("Dombas" is surely how you'll feel when trying to assemble the Dombas wardrobe cabinet), smaller text detailing the products, bold numbers indicating the price, the occasional bolded "NEW" beckoning. As with the customary sensory overload of an IKEA catalog, the eye does not know where to rest, there is too much information to take in, and the dizzying effect is worsened by the camera moving quickly. Moreover, the disorientation is heightened by the depth of field consequent upon the camera's distance from the interiors which exceeds their integral dimensions, in a way that reveals that the apartment is a set without a fourth wall. After completing almost the entire 360 degree, Edward Norton walks into the frame, effectuating the transformation from the two dimensionality of catalogue to the three dimensionality of film. The sequence renders Jack's apartment a perfect museum of his painstaking choices and their pre-ordained coordination. But it simultaneously renders the profession and labor of set design more perceptible, highlighting the material conditions of cinema by bringing the background to the foreground. Setting is an indispensable element of film form, yet lay spectators, film critics, and film theorists too often overlook it as merely the backdrop for charismatic performances or fancy camerawork. Set design isn't even an Oscar category. It is folded into art direction, which also includes overseeing costumes (even though that has its own Oscar), locations, and transportation.

This overlooked labor is called out in parallel as Jack's voice-over concludes the sequence:

If I saw something clever like a little coffee table in the shape of a yin-yang, I had to have it. The Klipske personal office unit, the Hovetrekke home exer-bike, or the Johannshamn sofa with the Strinne green stripe pattern. Even the Rizlampa wire lamps of environmentally friendly unbleached paper.

I'd flip through catalogs and wonder: What kind of dining set defines me as a person? I had it all. Even the glass dishes with tiny bubbles and imperfections. Proof that they were crafted by the honest, simple, hard-working indigenous peoples of

. . . . His narration is interrupted by a jarring audio splice back into the diegetic world: "(Operator) Please hold," reminding us again of the contrastive interplay with print and telephone technology that the sequence assembles. The jarring sensation renews as Jack reverts to narration, finishing his sentence ". . . wherever." He knows he is supposed to like the idea of the native craftsman in an exotic location, but he doesn't really care—or, more precisely, the system of intermedial relations (commodification, communications, marketing) that brings him into contact with that native simultaneously obscures any substantive details. Through the switching of registers between diegetic and voice-over, the switching of media between catalogue, telephone, and film, and the cinematography's switching between realism and artifice, the IKEA sequence uses form to call our attention to gaps between the commodity and the labor that produces it, whether that commodity is an air-bubbled glass dish or a Hollywood movie.

The unconventional perspective confabulated by the camerawork in the IKEA sequence is rivalled only by the film's inventive use of reverse-tracking shots blended with CGI. Four remarkable sequences work in this way, starting at an estranging microscopic level and reverse-tracking the images out toward a larger, more familiar scale: the opening credits (which we have already discussed)—with their merger of the celluloid, the logo, the industrial, and the molecular in the reverse from Jack's neural pathways out to his pores out to his position subjected to a pistol in Tyler's hand; the second sequence in the film; a sequence in a trashcan; and the flashback to the explosion which destroyed Jack's condo. The repetition of the maneuver signals the film's interest in foregrounding it.

Reverse-tracking is employed quite early in the film, in its second sequence. Pivoting from the opening gun-laden interaction between Tyler and the narrator in a dark, blue-lit space with large windows looking out on several skyscrapers, the camera jumps into the space outside. The fast-tracking shot moves from Tyler's gaze out the window, down the glass side of the building, through the pavement of the street, underground to a garage, inside a van and to the wired center of a bomb. Then the camera even more rapidly reverse tracks from this close-up through walls, up to the ground level, across streets, through other walls, and into similar spaces in other buildings, closing in on other bombs. In this instance, the technique literalizes in cinematographic form the fundamental gesture of Marxist critique establishing context for ideas. The formal trajectory of that critique—its movement from the specific to the general—is accentuated by the way this reverse-tracking echoes the camerawork in the opening credits.

Such motion recurs yet again in the trashcan scene, at an early moment we have already discussed regarding ideology: Jack is at work, staring in to space, lost in reverie about corporate domination, but his private thoughts make no difference to his actions as a worker keeping the system going. Ideology is what we do. Jack is shown standing at the copy machine, staring almost straight into the camera but with a vacant gaze, and then the image cuts to an inscrutable frame of white walls covered in brown splotches, bisected by a reddish-brown pipe. The camera reverses, but doesn't yet gain much perspective, navigating past other grimy rectangles and circles, some with embossed lettering, as Jack narrates "When deep space exploitation ramps up, it will be corporations that name everything." At the moment he says "corporations," the strange shapes become apparent as a Krispy Kreme package, a soda can, a White Castle carton (the narration continuing "The IBM Stellar Sphere. The Microsoft Galaxy") and finally an entire Starbucks cup, alone in the corner of a 4 cup to-go carrier, perched atop a trashcan ("Planet Starbucks"). Postproduction lore holds that this sequence was the very last to be finished for the film, expending tremendous effort. Notably, in employing the reverse-tracking form used in the opening credits, the trashcan sequence aligns its content with that of the credits: rapid transit through corporate logos and proper names, a solar system of brands shaping the world in the film just as it shapes the world of the film.

The importance of this reverse-tracking maneuver is built in to its conspicuous repetitive use. The apartment sequence is strategically repeated by the special camerawork of a flashback reconstructing the cause of the destruction of Jack's apartment. He has just returned from the business trip on which he has first met Tyler, and as the taxi pulls up he notes,

> Home was a condo on the fifteenth floor of a filing cabinet for widows and young professionals. The walls were solid concrete. A foot of concrete's important when your next-door neighbor lets her hearing aid go and has to watch gameshows at full volume, or when a volcanic blast of debris that used to be your furniture and personal effects blows out of your floor-to-ceiling windows and sails flaming into the night.

Lapsing into diegesis, Jack interacts with his doorman, surrounded by firefighters, and then resumes his narration, "The Police would later tell me that the pilot light might have gone out." From this later time, the film image cuts back to the apartment, and embarks on a striking sequence. The camera moves toward the stove, and then produces what is sometimes called "bullet time," after a famous scene using the technique in *The Matrix* in the same year as *Fight Club*. In bullet time, numerous stationary cameras arranged at 360 degrees around a scene each film a single shot, which are then edited together to simulate 360-degree camera movement in a rather unattainable perspective. The bullet time sequence encompasses a burner on the stove, and then the camera zooms in to the pilot flame, before commencing the reverse shot in the same style as the credits and the trashcan sequence, from the burner out into the kitchen airspace, and then renarrowing behind the fridge, toward the compressor. The explosion literalizes the impossibility for the narrator to continue on in the same vein. It serves as a cheesy plot device, a special effect redoubled by the sequence depicting the pilot light building up gas, the fridge compressor surging, a fireball engulfing the perfect IKEA spread.

These recurrent reverse shots highlight the construction of cinematic imagery and foreground the work of camera operators and editors. In their repetition, they reveal the mechanics by which a single film or even a director's oeuvre manufacture style. And in their vector outward from micro to macro, they perform the perspectival contextualization that characterizes Marxist analysis, from Marx's very first definition of materialism, onward. *Fight Club*'s signature stylized filmwork can be seen as the cinematic materialization of Marxism's signature interpretative procedure. And the film goes to lengths to further this association of the layering of multiple cameras into perspective with important contextualizing insights when it tries to attain an objective rendering of Jack's panic against Project Mayhem. At the very end of the film, as Jack frantically tries to undo the bomb plot, the camera tracks him running toward a van full of explosives in the target skyscraper's basement, and then cuts to closed-circuit security camera footage of a different vantage on the same scene. When Tyler joins Jack and they commence fist fighting, the closed-circuit depicts Jack fighting by himself, contrasting the film's deceptive official representation, with a different technology's capacity to picture a truth, but it also echoes the earlier revisionist scenes of the official camera revealing Jack alone in scenes that were previously shot with Tyler. The sequence also brilliantly refers to other pivotal ones in the film: the staged self-fight in the boss's office when Jack takes his "smirking revenge," and the footage of Jack fighting himself rather than Tyler, in the revision of their first fight that is replayed after the identity reveal. Toward the very end, when Jack shoots himself to try to eliminate Tyler, the gunshot merges with CGI of a blue light explosion and then smoke twirls upward; Tyler staggers, is ensconced in smoke, and disappears. Such repetitions foreground the film's repeated construction of relations and accentuate the power of the medium to mediate its own constructions.

Genre bending

If we are starting to recognize how the camerawork in the film focuses intently on the medium, we can now turn to consider how the film's overall genre contributes to this emphasis. *Fight Club* subjects the medium of film to scrutiny through its sophisticated wielding of genre. Genres are conventions for producing and consuming. They help filmmakers anchor their pitches ("it's buddy flick meets Star Wars!"), help marketers target audiences ("if you liked *Save the Last Dance* you'll love *Step Up!*"), and help audiences feel like savvy consumers ("I knew he'd get the girl in the end"). Common genres in film are horror, rom-com, action, espionage, and Westerns. Genres indicate parameters for themes (gangster), for style (detective, musical), for technique (slow-motion, soaring soundtrack). Filmmakers can use the parameters to shape their art, and audiences can use them to interpret art, including knowing what to expect before viewing a film, and evaluating it afterward. Genres can also be thought of as efficient communication, creating a common understanding between artists and audiences: you know what you're going to get, you know why a certain stock character type or stock plot development takes place, and you know that the director wants you to know this.

When films blend or contradict genres, they undo this efficient communication, creating opportunities for greater confusion and greater reflection. And when a film works through a succession of genres, it destabilizes the audience—each time you think you know what kind of movie you're in, the rug is pulled out from under you. Many films try to evade genres, and most films blend genres; how a film manages this push-and-pull of genre is worthy of analysis. *Fight Club* mediates the medium of film through its genre-bending and genre-shifting.

Fight Club is hard to classify in generic terms because it incorporates so many genres and moves through them almost successively. In the beginning, the film appears to be a satire, with a deadpan narrative and visual hyperbole marking the on-screen subjects for ridicule. When Jack meets Marla, it takes a turn as wonky romantic comedy. When he meets Tyler, and for most of the first hour, it seems to be a buddy picture, in which a charisma differential helps both men mature. When fight club takes off, the film starts to work as a parable of consumer society, and this continues when the club morphs into Project Mayhem. When Jack's relationships with Marla and Tyler are problematized and the big reveal takes place, the film positions itself in the genre of spectacular twister, in the tradition of *The Sixth Sense* or *The Usual Suspects*. And the confusing conclusion seems to return to romantic comedy, the most abiding Hollywood genre, yet the fact that the narrator has undergone a dramatic transformation from deadpan to happily, confidently engaged, against a backdrop of political destruction, seems to also reactivate the satire of the very beginning.

The most important effect of all of this shifting is to make the film into an interpretative problem. The shifting keeps us guessing as to what possible kinds of resolution will come down the pike, and as to how we should regard the characters. Are they romantic heroes we identify with, or grotesque caricatures we keep distance from? Is the tone one that encourages us to adopt Tyler's analysis of the capitalist mode of production, or that estranges us from this? In what sense does the ending tidily resolve the film's many conflicts? With its genre play, *Fight Club* reflects on and disrupts the conventionality of the Hollywood system. It thwarts the knowingness of audiences and critics, and courts their active engagement.

Intertextuality and the labor of cinema

As with its genre-bending, which puts the work of genre under the spotlight, *Fight Club*'s frequent references to other films or other filmic contexts also offer up the medium of film for reflections on how it functions. Intertextuality is both a hallmark of artsy Hollywood, and a surprising way that the film calls attention to the labor of its production. Intertextuality refers to the interweaving of texts—the ways that individual artworks enfold and entangle strands from other art works, the ways that works cite each other, the ways that works blur the boundaries of their uniqueness by incorporating, invoking, and inscribing other works. In cinema intertextuality can be as simple as a character quoting a signature line from another movie. It can be camerawork or set design quoting memorable sequences from another movie. It can be a relationship among sequels or franchises or remakes.

Almost all of these conventions of intertextuality operate in *Fight Club*. What is more, the film goes to significant lengths to make intertextual references that foreground the film industry itself, including references to other Fincher films, other films made by its cast, and to the collective work of making film. In the conventional vein, we can note references to other films in general. Shots of the outside of the Paper St house directly quote Hitchcock's composing of the Bates residence in *Psycho*. The camerawork in the "near-life experience" scene, especially the mounting of the camera on the outside of the car, starkly mimics David Cronenberg's *Crash*. When the character of Chloe is introduced, the narrator says, "Chloe looked the way Meryl Streep's skeleton would look if you made it smile and dance around the party being extra nice to everybody," a disturbing image which blends masterful performance, female mortality, and the diegetic reality of *Fight Club* with the extra-diegetic reality of Hollywood.

Other instances of intertextuality function more pointedly to highlight film labor by referring the characters back to the actors whose work is to play. In one of the film's only exterior sequences, as Jack puts Marla on a bus out of town, the set includes billboards and broadsides for other films in which *Fight Club* cast members had starred, most noticeably Brad Pitt's *Seven Years in Tibet*. As Marla, Helena Bonham Carter speaks a line almost identical to one she speaks as Katherine in her earlier film *Margaret's Museum*. In answer to why she attends support groups when she clearly doesn't suffer from testicular cancer, she says "It's cheaper than a movie, and there's free coffee." In the earlier film, her morbid character attends many funerals, and when asked "who died?" she replies "It don't matter. I go to 'em all. It's cheaper than bingo, and the grub is better." The fact that Marla specifically contrasts spectating the support groups with spectating movies also deepens the intertextual effect, prompting viewers to align their spectatorship of films about suffering alienation and committing self-destruction with Marla's voyeurism.

In similar fashion, Edward Norton's role as a leader of an uprising with populist overtones echoes the Oscar-nominated performance for which he was best known prior to *Fight Club*, in *American History X*. The films share grim style, shadowy cinematography, and several scenes of a shirtless Norton fighting or a bruised Norton looking in the mirror. One of the aliases that Jack adopts in attending the various support groups, displayed on his nightly nametags—Cornelius—alludes to a character in *Planet of the Apes*. Through such references, Edward Norton may be constructed as a type, but, more importantly, *Fight Club* constructs itself as a film made out of other films and the industrial web from which they are spun.

Beyond these intertextual references to the actors and their labor, *Fight Club* also incorporates references to set design, screenplay writing, and crew members. The scene of the very first fight between Jack and Tyler, outside Lou's bar, recreated in Wilmington, includes several shots of an early model brown station wagon. The car is the exact vehicle prop also used in Fincher's 1997 film *The Game*, for a sequence in which Michael Douglas hides in the car to sneak into CRS (Consumer Recreation Services). In both films, a CRS sticker is visible on the car's windshield. Fincher's earlier film *Seven* (1995) is also invoked by references to Andrew Kevin Walker, a *Fight Club* screenplay collaborator and *Seven* screenplay coauthor, for whom three detectives in the scene where Jack attempts to turn himself in are named (Detective Andrew, Detective Kevin, Detective Walker). Walker also had a cameo in *Seven*; the reference to his name in *Fight Club* highlights the labor of the many individuals cooperating in the production of film. Such appreciation is echoed in another moment in *Fight Club*, when Jack sits at his desk composing haikus of corporate alienation ("Worker bees can leave / even drones can fly away / the queen is their slave") to share with his coworkers. The long list of names of recipients in the "to" field of the email are crew members, whose names will again appear in long list during the closing credits.

In the opening of this chapter, we staged the tension between beginning a Marxist film analysis with film form and beginning with conditions of production. The way the film itself presents that tension, with its innovative credit sequence, is another site of its mediation of cinematic production. After the film's very first words, the camera continues the movement outward that apparently began inside Jack's cells, in the credit sequence that visually identifies biological cell structure with the celluloid of film. The film is producing its character, making him out of transparent plastic, and analogizing that production to material, organic processes. This interconnection of the biological and the psychological and the technological will recur throughout the film, which consistently describes corporeal and psychic experience in terms of their determination by economic relations. And, arguably, the credit sequence also makes this connection at another level, layering the names of individuals involved in making the film with the animated materials. As a whole, the credit sequence makes a formal articulation that the film's story also makes thematically: identities, whether "real" like "Edward Norton" or fictional like "Tyler Durden," and including the unconscious, are intertwined with material forces.

From the directors Hitchcock and Cronenberg to the screenplay writer Walker to the actors Carter and Norton, from set design and props to cinematographic techniques, from naming the generally unnamed crew to naming the household name Meryl Streep, these intertextual references summon some of the diverse types of labor that go in to producing a Hollywood film. *Fight Club*'s intertextuality therefore becomes a technique for its mediation of the cinematic mode of production, for its opening up of the relations between the unified illusion on the screen and the diversified labor that puts it there. Any evaluation of the film's attitude toward capitalism must reckon with these mediations, taking stock of just how thoroughly the film equips us to explore production, ideology, and the work of representation.

Splicing

In keeping with its intertextual references to the labor of acting, directing, writing, and set design, *Fight Club* strategically incorporates the labor of film editing and film projection. The most prominent strand here is Tyler's work as a projectionist. We have already discussed the splicing pranks he pulls there, but it is also quite important that when this job is introduced, the narrator and Tyler have something of a heterodiegetic conversation. The narrator says,

> He had one part time job as a projectionist. See, a movie doesn't come all on one big reel. It comes on a few. So someone has to be there to switch the projectors at the exact moment that one reel ends and the next one begins. If you look for it, you can see these little dots come into the upper right-hand corner of the screen.

Tyler interjects, "In the industry, we call them cigarette burns," and the narrator continues "That's the cue for a changeover. He flips the projectors, the movie keeps right on going, and nobody in the audience has any idea." The occluded labor of the projectionist is what enables the blissful ignorance of the audience illusion; the strange convergence of two narratives constitutes a meta-narrative that is required to puncture the illusion.

Cigarette burns are refigured in the film by the repeated, identical lye burns that members of Project Mayhem ritualistically incur off-screen. There is a decisive scene in which Tyler, while teaching Jack the formula for dynamite and the process for making soap, gives Jack a terrible burn on purpose as part of propelling him to "hit bottom." The shape of the burn scar is a very distinctive oval mimicking the cigarette burns, and marks numerous other characters throughout the film, without being made a subject of conversation. The burns link together the geographically disparate clubs that Jack visits as he reconstructs Tyler's political organizing, analogizing their function to that of the cigarette burn that signals the need for the projectionist to link reels. We might say that the work of editing and projecting is materialized within the diegesis in the burn mark; through this repeated imagery the film mediates the seams between its own diegetic and technological registers.

As Jack and Tyler continue to argue about whether they are the same person, Jack's denial takes over. Tyler stands up, points at Jack and declares, "You're insane. We simply do not have time for this crap," upon which Jack closes his eyes as if fainting and falls back on a bed. Edward Norton's voice-over relays, "It's called a changeover. The movie goes on and nobody in the audience has any idea." The confrontation doesn't get resolved, and the next frame shows Jack waking up in the same bed. The repetition almost verbatim of the earlier didactic scene about changeover technology reinforces the entwining of the psychic revelation and medium literacy, constructing a parallelism between Jack's inability to accept the reality of his dissociations and the cinema-goer's ignorance of the technological artifice. Conversely, to know that Jack's dissociative disorder is the propagation of an ideal image is also to know that films are labor-intensive machines for image-making. Tyler looks like Jack wants to look; Jack has learned what to look like from the moving picture industry.

The laborious editing I mentioned in accounting for the empirical conditions of production of the film results in some of the film's greatest technical genius and most sophisticated formal creativity. Specifically, *Fight Club* makes extensive use of splicing, the insertion of noncontinuous frames into the middle of a reel, in order to leave hints of its ultimate reveal and to call attention to the medium of film. For example, within the story the film tells, Tyler is a laborer who responds to boredom at work with clever pranks; one such prank involves sabotaging his job as a commercial projectionist by splicing frames of pornography into children's films. Later *Fight Club* itself performs this exact prank, inserting a close-up of male genitals amid the film's closing sequence. Throughout the film, four shots of Brad Pitt are spliced into scenes of Edward Norton, providing flashes of their shared identity. The first one occurs while the narrator is describing how his inability to sleep is challenging his reality: "With insomnia, nothing is real. . . . Everything is a copy of a copy of a copy." The scene is the copy room in his office, but there is a split-second spliced image of Brad Pitt. The others include the hallway of the doctor's office where Jack has sought insomnia medication, the testicular cancer support group meeting, and a streetscape as he watches Marla walk away.

The film's closing sequences includes a marvelous meta-moment, as the final shots of the film, framing Jack and Marla, holding hands, looking each other in the eye, against the skyscraper demolition, are interrupted with a spliced in full-frontal penis shot in the penultimate second. This stroke of editing marries the world in which Tyler labors as a projectionist, sabotaging family films with porn, to the world in which spectators of *Fight Club* consume the film. Switching levels between diegetic and extra-diegetic in this way, the film insistently mediates its own conditions of production.

As the film's form thematizes the art and labor of editing, it also repeats this switching of level when it takes on a new form for home consumption. The DVD version of the film, which we have already noted has been unusually successful, profitable, and lauded, opens with the standard FBI warning against pirating which all DVDs make impossible to fast-forward. Directly after this, Fincher inserts a fake second FBI warning, on the same background and font as the first, continuous with the first, declaring, among other things:

> If you are reading this then this warning is for you. Every word you read of this useless fine print is another second off your life. Don't you have other things to do? Is your life so empty that you honestly can't think of a better way to spend these moments? Or are you so impressed with authority that you give respect and precedence to all who claim it. . . . Quit your job. Start a fight. Prove you're alive. If you don't claim your humanity, you will become a statistic. You have been warned . . . . Tyler.

This parody fulfills an intent Fincher had, to tweak the corporate logos in the opening sequence to contain subliminal messages or ironic iconography. The studios denied permission. But the remediation of the DVD provided the opportunity to integrate the film's diegetic reflections on conformity, obedience, and ideological everyday doings with the spectatorial universe of film consumption.

Narration

The DVD warning hails the spectator with its use of the second person pronoun "you." Throughout the film, Tyler makes several speeches in the second person. One of the film's most famous and reproduced moments is a second-person address from Tyler, alone in a room but speaking to a you: "You are not how much money you have in the bank. You're not the car you drive. You're not the contents of your wallet." He then turns and looks directly into the camera, combining the second-person interpellation with the fourth-wall break: "You're not your fucking khakis. You are the all-singing all-dancing crap of the world." In this way the film uses the technology of voice-over and a technique of medium-conspicuousness to model the process of political organizing: in order to join a movement, individuals need to recognize what the collective holds in common, and need to stand at some distance from the normal middle of things. The medium's self-awareness, puncturing its own illusions, is both catalyst and exemplar; the second-person address, building affiliations, is both jarring and compelling. Losing your illusions, recognizing the common—these are processes of "consciousness raising" that are integral to social struggle.

This brings us to the most unusual feature of the film's formal composition, the epicenter of its form system: it is *narrated*. In our discussion of media theory, we noted Marshall McLuhan's dictum that new media define themselves in terms of the media they succeed. Prior to film, the great popular medium was the novel, which is defined in large part by its narrativity: a discursive relay of its diegetic world. Film does not require narration since the camera can confabulate a world visually without discourse, using cinematography to relay context in establishing shots or priority in close-ups. In instances when a film is constructed with a narrator, it is therefore important to ask why the form plays out this way.

The form of the voice-over is a highly unusual choice, and it was not employed in the first versions of the screenplay. Fincher fought for this perspective, which he had not used before and did not use again until *Gone Girl* (2014). The great director Stanley Kubrick noted that voice-over is usually a symptom of a problem in a script, but he also noted that "when thoughts are to be conveyed, especially when they are of a nature which one would not say to another person, there is no other good alternative."[6] The voice-over introduces the problematic element to foreground the limits of visual filmic representation: sometimes a different level of discourse is necessary to grapple with the complexities at stake. In this way, the form of cinematic voice-over aestheticizes the contradictory character of situated perspective that we have seen to inspire Marx's original critique of the ruling ideas of the ruling class, as well as the contradiction between the visual and the verbal/ the imaginary and the symbolic, that fuels ideology.

Crucially, *Fight Club*'s strategy for indicating these limits is subjective: it doesn't employ objective narration, but rather a narrator who speaks in the first person, using first-person pronouns, providing his personal account of events in which he also takes part. This voice-over function produces an interesting tension with the often-constructed omniscience or objectivity of the camera's point of view in Hollywood conventions. Jack is not present in every scene, so the camera creates access to perspectives that are not his—it creates a rival narration. This rivalry is compounded by the dynamic we have already noted, of Tyler's quasi-narrative function in his long speeches and direct address to the camera. We might say that *Fight Club* is interested in a deep, formal way in the problem of point of view, of how to narrate social and psychological experience under the capitalist mode of production, of whether individuals can know their own social and psychic realities. The film uses its formal components to array this problem. Subjectivity, the voice-over choice suggests, is situated at the junction of the imaginary and the symbolic, an ideological interpellation that can also become the site of new relations.

Narration in the first person by a character involved in the action always faces the problem of time: the relation between the time of narrating and the time of narration. From its very beginning, *Fight Club* employs flashback to address this problem. After the opening sequence's reflections on where to start, the narrative engages in hugely self-reflexive mediating gestures that underline the film's constructedness. The Narrator identifies Pitt's character as Tyler and reveals that they are about to witness Project Mayhem. The Narrator says, "I know this because Tyler knows this," indicating that, despite the gun, he and Tyler have an intimate connection. The Narrator offers context for the conflict between himself and Tyler and Project Mayhem's imminent "destruction" by saying, "Then suddenly I realize that all of this—the guns, the bombs, the revolution, has got something to do with a girl named Marla Singer." The Narrator dictates the cut to the second scene through telling the audience directly to back up. Next shown at a meeting of a testicular cancer support group, the Narrator explains that he had begun attending support group meetings in order to alleviate his own emotional alienation and insomnia. He once again makes direct reference to the filmic apparatus by saying "Wait, back up again" and reverting to an earlier scene to provide yet more context. Conventional Hollywood narrative constructs an omniscient perspective for the spectator, but *Fight Club*'s self-conscious storytelling happens through a different, though no less standardized, single narrator perspective. When the film catches up with itself after its enormous flashback, Jack's voice-over notes, "I think this is about where we came in," and Tyler repeats his question from the opening: "Would you like to say a few words to mark the occasion?" But whereas in the opening Jack had said, "I can't think of anything," in the ending he says, "I still can't think of anything," and Tyler replies, "Ah, flashback humor." Breaking the fourth wall, this joke acknowledges the temporal lag between the flashback and the present, incorporating the spectatorial experience into its own dialogue.

The narrator in *Fight Club* develops a signature move that serves to highlight another medium faculty of film. He repeatedly, nearly a dozen times, speaks in the formula, "I am Jack's___" to describe his feelings: "I am Jack's Raging Envy," "I am Jack's Inflamed Sense of Rejection." These statements crystallize the narrator's deadpan style in ways that reinforce his account of himself as unable to experience significant affect or to engage in meaningful connections. They also manufacture style from the friction among mediums, the fact that the medium of film does not use the same techniques as written fiction to unlock the achievement of literary narration: presenting a character's interiority, their inner thoughts and feelings. Like the theater, film relies upon actors to externalize inner states through gestures, expressions, tone. Unlike the theater, film can add shot structure (close-up, down-shot, up-shot, etc.) to amplify and frame these externalizations. But neither film nor theater can directly relay to the audience a description of the character's thoughts. *Fight Club*'s narrator can do this, especially because he employs the first person. But rather than authenticate that relay, the film makes such moments into a slogan, a gimmick, a copy: Jack appropriates the formula from an old magazine about anatomy. Remarking that the Paper St house's previous owner was "a bit of a shut-in," the camera scans large stacks of magazines, finding Jack reading by flashlight. He calls out, "Listen to this. It's an article written by an organ in the first person. I am Jack's medulla oblongata. Without me Jack could not regulate his heart rate, blood pressure, or breathing." In this moment, the film evokes another medium, print magazines, and the weirdness of the aesthetic mode of first-person narration, which it has already been itself employing. The formula provides a tagline for the film that fuels its cult sensibility (you can still to this day buy T-shirts that say "I am Jack's medulla oblongata"), that offers "Jack" as a useful name for the previously unnamed narrator, and that marks the interrelation between different media forms, the continuity of narrative media forms. This is part of the film's systematic effort to think about how image production constructs fantasies, and how medium awareness enables critical distance from those fantasies.

Fight Club's voice-over problematizes itself even further by mixing its first-person narration with second-person narration, and by employing more than one first-person narrator. Jack hails the audience: "You wake up at SeaTac, SFO, LAX. . . . Lose an hour, gain an hour. This is your life, and it's ending one minute at a time. . . . If you wake up at a different time, in a different place, could you wake up as a different person?"

Such questions directly hail the spectator, effectuating a verbal break in the fourth wall. Sometimes the second person is employed by Jack, sometimes by Tyler, but in both cases the interpellation positions viewers to envision themselves as part of the movement *Fight Club* chronicles, as participating in the structure of feeling and courses of action it represents.

In parallel, Tyler is not the film's main narrator, but he does use both the second-person and the first-person plural at charged moments. In his first social interaction with Jack, over a drink Jack initiates after his condo explosion, Tyler addresses Jack but also addresses the spectator: "It's all going down. I say never be complete. I say stop being perfect. Let's evolve; let the chips fall where they may." His exhortation is soon followed by his imperative to Jack: "Hit me as hard as you can"—and thus begins their first fight. Later, Tyler addresses a large crowd at the club, a stump speech whose revolving 360-degree shot composition and collective pronouns work to encompass the audience:

> Advertising has us chasing cars and clothes, working jobs we hate so we can buy shit we don't need. We are the middle children of history, man. No purpose or place. We have no Great War. No Great Depression. Our Great War is a spiritual war, our Great Depression is our lives. We've all been raised on television to believe that one day we'd all be millionaires, and movie gods, and rock stars. But we won't. And we're slowly learning that fact. And we're very, very pissed off.

Such moments begin with him on screen, but they often blend into voice-over narration of the type originally used in the film by Edward Norton's voice. This is one of many small techniques the film uses to formally identify Tyler and Jack well before it has done so in the plot. But the content of these monologues is also important. The character is directly taking on the role of narrator, explaining the world within the film, and using language that also leaps out to explain the world outside of the film. In the example above, the explanations incriminate the media: advertising and television and movies and music instill illusory beliefs that the masses will eventually be powerful, successful, wealthy. The author John Steinbeck famously said that the reason there has been no socialist or communist revolution in the United States is because "we didn't have any self-admitted proletarians. Everyone was a temporarily embarrassed capitalist." Tyler's monologue imagines a process of disillusionment, when this temporary embarrassment is recognized as a permanent social fact. Yet at the same time, the film's pointing to the cinema's role in perpetuating the illusion means we might also question what new illusion arises when the illusion is revealed.

Unending

Hollywood narrative conventions prioritize the objectivity of narration, the agency of characters, and closure or resolution. The conflicts that drive the story tend to wind up solved in some fashion at the end of the film, alleviating the tension that the conflicts stir up. Conventions for closure include classic literary tropes like marriage or death, action tropes like a villain coming to justice, and restoration tropes that return a family, a town, or a workplace to normalcy after a threat, trial, transformation. *Fight Club* wrestles with all of these conventions, in its subjective narration, its agency of the social, and its refusal of closure. Its final shot dramatically relays what can only be the beginning of a new phase of Project Mayhem, the explosion of corporate headquarters in almost a dozen skyscrapers. Even if all the members of the project are immediately arrested, this large blow will generate media attention, public efforts at understanding, and reverberating consequences for companies and individuals. Jack takes Marla's hand and reassures her that "everything is going to be fine." The final shot captures silhouettes of the Narrator and Marla, holding hands, framed by the demolitions. The ending does not provide closure of a conventional sort, but rather introduces new turns in the plot that incentivize repeated viewing of the film, and that open a number of pathways for a sequel to be produced.

The conclusion of the film involves the emergence of Jack as a new subject, the establishment of a new, direct relationship with Marla, and the new state of affairs created by the destruction. All this novelty and the promise therein is accentuated by the closing sequence's decidedly upbeat tone. The camerawork takes broader shots than in much of the film, offering a sense of expanse. At the same time, this expanse is rooted in squarely framed context, since the final shots are some of the very few establishing shots with exterior settings in the entire film. The lighting is blue cast, more positive than the dark shadows and unnerving yellows of most of the film. And the music is irrepressibly upbeat, "Where Is My Mind?" a 1988 track from the Pixies from their debut *Surfer Rosa*, long recognized as one of the greatest rock albums of all time.

For Marx, one benefit of the materialist approach to history as contingent rather than inevitable was a corollary approach to the present as in process rather than as fixed. *Fight Club* punctuates this ongoingness of the present by juxtaposing a radical social event, the demolition of the financial center, with the more intimate and banal events of psychic reintegration and romantic connection. Contradictions remain in motion. At psychic, interpersonal, and political levels, new sets of relations unfurl toward the future.

Conclusion

Films engage our desires, educate us about this world and possible worlds, and entertain us in between the hours of the working day. Indeed, one of the most powerful aspects of cinematic experience is the way its immersiveness (and, until recently, its location in the theater) generally means that we cannot work while doing it. The time of the cinema is the time of leisure, of play, of producing things other than calculable value. Many professions and jobs enable listening to music while working, but few enable watching movies. This exception from the normal rhythms of daily life and normal imperatives of productivity make film a site of ambiguous political meaning. On the one hand, as we have reviewed in this book, Hollywood films are produced industrially with enormous budgets by major studios for global consumption. The economic interests of the industry tend toward return of these significant investments, and toward sustaining the economic system that makes them possible. Small wonder, then, that so many films would seem readily readable as expressions of capitalist values. On the other hand, as we have also analyzed, the medium of film requires collective practice, the consumption of cultural texts often sparks the formation of critical consciousness, the experience of watching film demands that we make time for not working, and the prominence of film provides avenues for sociability and solidarity. It would be a poor theory of film to hold it in only one of these two hands. Marxism does not commend both-sides-ism, but it models dialectics, the ability to grasp contradictions. Holding a film in both hands, we can see how its contradictions mediate the contradictions of capitalism. *Fight Club* thematizes these contradictions, but beyond that, its form works to repeatedly reveal the contradictions between mediation and ideology, between representation and social reproduction, between film and itself. Studying this film is an opportunity for studying contradictions, the ultimate Marxist analytic project.

Throughout this book we have tried to balance formal analysis with analysis of politico-economic conditions, attending especially to how forms themselves analyze political economy, to how texts produce their own contexts, to how cinematic production mediates the capitalist mode of production. Practicing this balance is the real charge of Marxist theory, and it is hard, which perhaps explains why there is so much film analysis which only operates one side of the equation. Achieving this balance requires navigating interpretative and methodological problems at every juncture, from how to start analysis (with intrinsic formal description or with extrinsic facts of production) to whether a cultural product can itself theorize. The willingness to approach film criticism, film analysis, and film theory as fallible, ongoing, situated practices—as questions not answers, as engaging processes rather than aggrandizing recipes—makes dialectical Marxist film theory a social relation and social practice that exists on a continuum with the social practice of film. Far from an authoritative, definitive explanation of film, Marxist film theory is an exercise in interpretation that keeps changing as its context evolves, that keeps illuminating as it proceeds. This is doubtless a frustrating point for a textbook to make, but my aim is to leave the reader with more questions than answers. Through the activity of questioning we can continue to situate our interpretations, repeating the elementary Marxist gesture of contextualizing ideas, and we can continue to attend to contradictions, upholding the fundamental Marxist theory of social relations.

Periodizing *Fight Club*

Fight Club came out twenty years ago. Yet far from feeling dated, it has become a contemporary classic because it so deftly weaves together film form and film theory: it uses formal self-reflexivity and formal inventiveness to explore how film partakes of a broader culture of image production that generates ideology at the same time as it mediates ideology. This mediating capacity means that *Fight Club* has lent itself to significant re-interpretation with every shift in the politico-economic landscape since its debut (the dot-com bubble, 9/11, the global financial crisis of 2007–2008, Occupy Wall Street, the great recession, globally insurgent white-supremacist nationalism). If the film's technical exuberance and political experimentation are enabled by the largess of the 1990s boom era in which it was made, its alienation from the hollows of consumerism and corporate calculating ring even stronger after the dot-com bubble burst. Its questioning of agency, its convocation of collectives, and its demolition of towers seem ominous and prescient after 9/11. Its critique of commodity culture may not resonate with millennials, who have traded stuff for experiences, but its targeting of the credit economy surely does. "If we erase the debt record, then we all go back to zero" rings as a moral imperative in this decade of prohibitive student debt and astronomical health care debt. Its opposition between blue-collar workers and service industry workers on the one side and the financial industry on the other is even more illuminating after the crisis of 2008 and the movement whose only demand was "we are the 99%." Its completely white cast seems an even bigger hole in its representation of capitalism amid the intensified contradictions of racialization in the twenty-first century. Minimalist consumption, collective labor for essentials like cooking and cleaning and housing, and the collaborative endeavor to radically change the world seem less menacingly cultish and more practically inevitable in the moment of rapidly extremizing climate change. The difference between physical fights and strategic projects is only heightened by the polarizing class war in the jobless recovery and the fascist upturn. In each new moment of capitalist contradiction, *Fight Club* offers ideas with which to map contradiction.

Across all those moments, across the very broad range of political ideas the film might be said to articulate, there is a consistency in the form's inventions and interventions, its stylized mobilization of the medium to call attention to itself. *Fight Club*'s fascination with image projection, the film industry, the labor of editing, and the production of illusion situate film as a social practice within the broad context of the capitalist mode of production, its ideologies, and its mediations. This link it forges between the formal and the political-economic is an overarching principle of Marxist theory which endures across the expanse of twenty years and shifting history.

Whence we write

The very first sentence of this book refers to the Marxist imperative to ask about the place from which something is being known. Critique of a film must reflect on the situation of critique in parallel to the situation of production. From where does a critic write? What is happening in the film critic's economy at the time they are making sense of the film? Why is the critic writing? Are they being paid to write a review for *Entertainment Weekly*? Are they writing for free for *Fandango* or the *Los Angeles Review of Books*? Are they writing a film theory textbook for professional laurels? The act of critical analysis can itself be subject to similar limits as the act of artistic production. Dialectical criticism acknowledges these limits.

Within these limits, critique is a practice of drawing connections between the overdeterminations of text and context and the utopian projection of alternatives. In this way interpretation must be kept open as a social practice, and the proper object of ideology critique must be kept in sight: ideology critique should not be the condemnation of an artwork for functioning ideologically—for how could it not? Instead it is the mapping, with the help of the art object, of the ideological structuring of the social relations which the critic aspires to transform. It is an active process in which critique is not a merely academic exercise but is an engaged way of being in the world, striving for a better world.

Writing this in the summer of 2018—when it is clear that the United States cannot pretend to lead the world, that the violence exercised upon black and brown bodies by police and border facilities is poorly containing the contradiction between a superelite class and the dispossessed masses, that the richest man in the world, worth $150 billion, steals his wealth from the 2.3 million employees driven under extreme productivity mandates to urinate in bottles, miscarry pregnancies on the warehouse floor, and routinely call ambulances for help breathing—it is hard not to look anywhere and everywhere for tactical support in movement building. Films do not by themselves change the world, but when they provide opportunities to watch together and learn together, and when they do so as intensely as *Fight Club*, their projective technology can spark imaginative projections of tactics and strategies, of different imaginary relations to different real conditions of production.

The Marxist film theorist attends to form and context, to the connections between the technology of the motion picture and the epistemology of Marxist critique, to the ways that film, as an integrated art, is very complicated to produce, and is disposed to understand the mode of production. It is a way of thinking about films, a way of thinking with films, a way of thinking about the capitalist mode of production. It is also a kind of critique, a thinking that aims to spur more than thinking—to spur utopian imaginings, to spur collective undertakings, to spur humane buildings. In this respect again, Marxist film theory shares something with film itself: they are both about motion, about action, about the hard work that turns inspiration into moving. Marxism grasps social structures not only to fathom the past and present but also to project a future; the medium of film also operates this positive projective horizon.

Marxist film theory equips teachers and students, writers and readers, filmmakers and spectators to move through everyday life in the highly visually saturated landscape of twenty-first-century capitalism. It links pleasures to production and social reproduction; it links our great escapes to our ongoing exploitation; it links representation to action; it links art to contradiction. The goal of Marxist film theory is to empower film spectators to approach film dialectically, ramifying the possibilities of its social influence in both destructive and emancipatory ways.

The last rule of Marxist film theory

Most film theory textbooks adopt an agnostic tone toward the panoply of options they present. Having produced a menu, they leave the reader free to order. You want feminist film theory, with a side of auteurism? You got it! Film theory is described as a neutral tool, to be deployed in varying contexts, and the competing approaches are presented as equally valid. Marxist film theory casts some doubts over this pluralist smorgasbord. As we have seen since the beginning of this book, Marxism directs our attention to the social power and social context of ideas, whether we understand "ideas" to mean the creative representation in the cinema or the critical analysis of that representation. Ideas are not neutral. A Marxist film theory textbook therefore cannot conclude with the beneficent instruction to go forth and make of it what you will, using it to spice up your buffet combo of postcolonial theory and reception theory and media theory alike. Instead, the Marxist practice of the dialectic and the Marxist commitment to the fundamental problematics of the mode of production, ideology, and mediation necessitate taking a stand. Marxist film theory is the best.

NOTES

Introduction

1 G. W. F. Hegel, *The Science of Logic* (New York: Prometheus Books, 1991), 56.

2 Riccioto Canudo, "The Birth of a Sixth Art," trans. B. Gibson, D. Ranvaud, S. Sokota, and D. Young in *French Film Theory and Criticism*, vol. 1, 1907–1929 (Princeton: Princeton University Press, 1988), 59.

3 Robert Stam, *Film Theory: An Introduction* (London: Wiley-Blackwell, 2000), 21.

Chapter one

1 Karl Marx, *Capital*, vol. 1 (New York: Penguin, 1992), 494.

2 I borrow this description from a longer expository piece I have written on "The German Ideology" for *The Bloomsbury Companion to Marx* (New York: Bloomsbury, 2019).

3 The argument over the next few pages is developed at length in my book *The Order of Forms*.

4 Caroline Levine, "Model Thinking: Generalization, Political Form, and the Common Good," *New Literary History* 48.4 (2017): 633.

5 I first formulated some of these ideas, and elaborated them at greater length, in my essay "We Have Never Been Critical: Toward the Novel as Critique" for *Novel: A Forum on Fiction* 50.3 (2017): 397–408.

6 Marx, *Capital*, 284.

7 https://www.marxists.org/archive/marx/works/1875/gotha/.

8   Grundrisse intro.

9   Sigmund Freud, *The Interpretation of Dreams* (New York: Basic Books, 2010), 266.

10 Karl Marx, *Contribution to the Critique of Political Economy* (New York: International, 1970).

11 Marx, *Capital*, 711.

12 For more on this French intellectual history, see "Ideology from Destutt De Tracy to Marx Emmet Kennedy," *Journal of the History of Ideas* 40.3 (1979): 353–68.

13 Marx, *Contribution to the Critique*.

14 Karl Marx, *The German Ideology* (New York: Prometheus, 1998), 42.

15 Hebert Marcuse, *One-Dimensional Man* (New York: Beacon Press, 1991), 130.

16 Antonio Gramcsi, *The Prison Notebooks* (New York: International Publishers, 1971), 165.

17 Louis Althusser and Etienne Balibar, *Reading Capital* (London: Verso, 2009), 28.

18 Ibid.

19 Matthew Flisfeder makes the argument that Žižek's work reveals that film studies ought to be a subset of the study of ideology. *The Symbolic, the Sublime, and Slavoj Žižek's Theory of Film* (London: Palgrave, 2012).

20 Tom Bottomore provides the most comprehensive overview of this philosophical lineage in *A Dictionary of Marxist Thought* (Cambridge: Harvard University Press, 1983), 373–75.

21 Marx, *The German Ideology*.

22 Theodor Adorno, "Thesen zur Kunstsoziologie," cited in Raymond Williams, *Marxism and Literature* (Oxford: Oxford University Press, 1978), 98.

23 Theodor Adorno, "Letter to Benjamin of 10 November 1938," *New Left Review* 81 (1973): 71. https://newleftreview.org/article/download_pdf?id=14.

24 Theodor Adorno, *Hegel: Three Studies* (Cambridge, MA: MIT Press, 1999), 57.

25 Williams, *Marxism and Literature*, 97–98.

26 Nathan Hensley, *Forms of Empire: The Poetics of Victorian Sovereignty* (Oxford: Oxford University Press, 2016), 17.

27 Richard Grusin, "Radical Mediation," *Critical Inquiry* 42.1 (2015): 147.

28 Catherine Gallagher, "Marxism and the New Historicism," Harold Vesser editor *The New Historicism* (London: Routledge, 1989), 42.

29 Sergei Eistenstein, *Film Sense* (San Diego: Harcourt, 1969), 91.

30 Theodor Adorno, *Minima Moralia* (New York: Verso, 1978), 206.

31 David Bordwell and Noel Carroll, *Post-Theory: Reconstructing Film Studies* (Madison: University of Wisconsin Press, 1996).

32 Sigfried Kracauer, *Theory of Film* (Princeton: Princeton University Press, 1997), 297, 299.

33 Letter to Harkness, April 1888, https://www.marxists.org/archive/marx/works/1888/letters/88_04_15.htm.

34 Stam, *Film Theory*, 73.

35 Philip Rosen, ed., *Narrative, Apparatus, Ideology* (New York: Columbia University Press, 1986), 447.

36 Christian Metz, *The Imaginary Signifier* (Bloomington: Indiana University Press, 1986), 51.

37 Ella Shohat and Robert Stam, *Unthinking Eurocentrism* (London: Routledge, 2014), 104.

38 Nathan Brown, "Postmodernity Not Yet," *Radical Philosophy* 2.01 (2018). https://www.radicalphilosophy.com/article/postmodernity-not-yet.

39 Fredric Jameson, *The Political Unconscious* (Ithaca: Cornell University Press, 1982), 296.

40 http://entertainment.time.com/2013/08/01/hey-america-entertainment-just-made-you-hundreds-of-dollars-richer/ and https://www.hollywoodreporter.com/news/hollywood-creative-industries-add-504-662691.

41 Jonathan Culler, *Literary Theory: A Very Short Introduction* (Oxford: Oxford University Press, 2011), 67.

Chapter two

1   Art Linson, *What Just Happened* (New York: Grove Press, 2008).

2   Associated Press, September 10, 1999.

3   https://www.nytimes.com/2009/11/08/movies/homevideo/08lim. html.

4   Marx, *Capital*, 926.

5   Slavoj Žižek, *Revolution at the Gates* (London: Verso, 2002), 252.

6   Interview with Michael Ciment, 1983, http://www.visual-memory. co.uk/amk/doc/interview.aco.html.

FURTHER READING

Roland Barthes, *Mythologies* (New York: Farrar, Straus and Giroux, 1972). Essay collection on meaning-making in everyday life, by the giant of semiology.

John Berger, *Ways of Seeing* (New York: Penguin, 1990). A highly pedagogical and visual introduction to the ideological critique of images.

Clint Burnham, *Fredric Jameson and The Wolf of Wall Street* (New York: Bloomsbury, 2016). A sibling book in this Bloomsbury series, covering the work of the greatest living Marxist film theorist.

Sergei Eisenstein, *Film Form* (San Diego: Harcourt, 1949). The first, and unsurpassed, theory of the medium from a Marxist perspective.

Fredric Jameson, *Signatures of the Visible* (New York: Routledge, 1992). Collects all of Jameson's early essays on cinema.

Fredric Jameson, *The Geopolitical Aesthetic* (Bloomington: Indiana University Press, 1995). Studies the spatial form of 70's cinema as it mediates globalization.

Annie McClanahan, *Dead Pledges* (Palo Alto: Stanford University Press, 2016). Includes analysis of horror films of the post-2008 era which illuminate the ideology of debt.

Todd McGowan, *Capitalism and Desire* (New York: Columbia University Press, 2016). The ultimate study of the linkage between psychic formations and the capitalist mode of production, greatly expanding the insights *Fight Club* proffers.

Michael Ryan and Douglas Kellner, *Camera Politica* (Bloomington: Indiana University Press, 1988). Considers film as a site of social struggle, paying attention to Hollywood representation that responds to the 1960s and 1970s social movements.

Ignacio Sanchez Prado, *Screening Neoliberalism* (Nashville: Vanderbilt University Press, 2015). Charts the absorption of Mexico's radical Marxist film theory and practice into its global market.

Mike Wayne, ed., *Understanding Film: Marxist Perspectives* (New York: Pluto Press, 2005). The only anthology devoted to explicitly Marxist film analysis.

Slavoj Žižek, *The Pervert's Guide to Ideology* (Zeitgeist Films, 2013). A DVD that teaches Marxist–Psychoanalytic ideology critique by studying film form and the circulation of tropes.

INDEX